FUN BIBLE Crosswords FOR KIDS

BARBOUR
PUBLISHING

Puzzles have previously appeared in *Kids' Bible Crosswords*.

Scripture quotations are taken from the HOLY BIBLE, NEW INTERNATIONAL VERSION®. NIV®. Copyright© 1973, 1978, 1984 by International Bible Society. Used by permission of Zondervan. All rights reserved.

Published by Barbour Publishing, Inc., P.O. Box 719, Uhrichsville, Ohio 44683, www.barbourbooks.com

Our mission is to publish and distribute inspirational products offering exceptional value and biblical encouragement to the masses.

ecpa Member of the
Evangelical Christian
Publishers Association

Printed in the United States of America.
Offset Paperback Mfrs., Inc., Dallas, PA; Print Code D10002168; January 2010

CREATION

GENESIS 1:1 - 2:3

ACROSS

1) ON THE 7th DAY GOD _____.
2) GOD MADE MAN FROM _____.
3) GOD MADE _____ FIRST.
4) MADE IN GOD'S IMAGE.

DOWN

1) EVE WAS MADE FROM ADAM'S _____.
5) THE FIRST WOMAN
6) THE GARDEN OF _____.
7) GOD CREATED EVERYTHING IN _____ DAYS.
8) THE FIRST MAN.

CAIN AND ABEL

GENESIS 4:1-17

ACROSS

1) ABEL WAS SHEPHERD OVER HIS _____.
2) CAIN WAS A _____.
3) CAIN'S FIRST SON WAS NAMED _____.
4) CAIN WAS SO ANGRY THAT HE _____ HIS BROTHER ABEL.

DOWN

5) CAIN ASKED GOD, "AM I MY BROTHER'S _____?".
6) AFTER ABEL'S MURDER, CAIN AND HIS WIFE _____ FAR AWAY FROM ADAM & EVE.
7) ADAM & EVE'S SECOND SON.
8) GOD PUT A _____ ON CAIN TO PROTECT HIM.
9) ADAM & EVE'S FIRST SON.

ANIMALS ON THE ARK

GENESIS 7:8

ACROSS

1) LARGE, STRONG CATTLE - "STRONG AS AN ___ "
2) SMALL RODENT THAT LIKES CHEESE.
3) HAS A POCKET AND HOPS
4) HAS A LONG NECK
5) HAS A HORN ON ITS NOSE
6) FASTEST ANIMAL ON LAND

DOWN

2) PRIMATES WITH TAILS
7) A _____ RETURNED TO NOAH WITH AN OLIVE BRANCH.
8) LARGE, WILD DOG
9) HOPS AND HAS BIG EARS, LOVES CARROTS
10) THE "KING OF BEASTS"
11) HAS A HUMP ON ITS BACK
12) LARGE, FLIGHTLESS BIRD

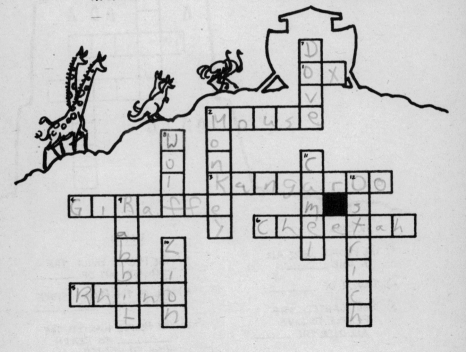

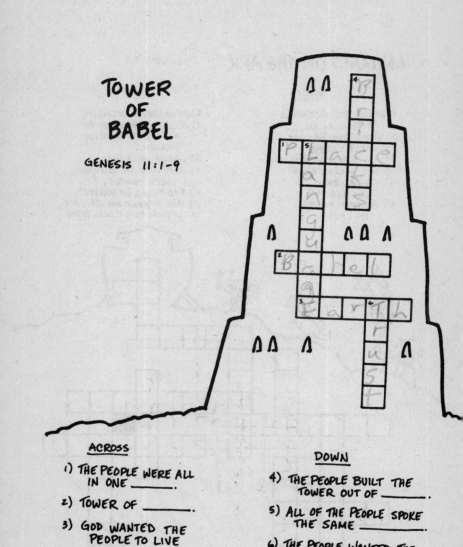

TOWER OF BABEL

GENESIS 11:1-9

ACROSS

1) THE PEOPLE WERE ALL IN ONE _____.

2) TOWER OF _____.

3) GOD WANTED THE PEOPLE TO LIVE ALL OVER THE _____.

DOWN

4) THE PEOPLE BUILT THE TOWER OUT OF _____.

5) ALL OF THE PEOPLE SPOKE THE SAME _____.

6) THE PEOPLE WANTED THE _____ TO REACH HIGH TO HEAVEN.

4

CANAAN, THE NEW LAND

GENESIS 13:5-18

ACROSS

1) THERE WAS NOT ENOUGH GREEN _____ FOR ALL THE SHEEP AND CATTLE TO EAT.

2) ABRAM + LOT COULD NOT _____ THE SAME LAND.

3) LOT WENT TO LIVE NEAR THE _____ RIVER.

DOWN

2) LOT WENT TO LIVE IN THIS WICKED CITY.

4) THE NEW LAND GOD BROUGHT ABRAM TO.

5) ABRAM AND LOT HAD FLOCKS OF THESE WOOLY ANIMALS.

6) ABRAM'S NEPHEW.

ABRAM BECOMES ABRAHAM

GENESIS 16, 17

ACROSS

1) ABRAM'S NEW NAME.

2) A MESSENGER FROM GOD.

3) GOD SAID SARAH WOULD HAVE A _____ BOY.

DOWN

4) ABRAHAM'S WIFE'S NEW NAME.

5) SARAH'S HANDMAID.

6) GOD SAID ABRAHAM WOULD BE THE FATHER OF _____ NATIONS.

7) _____ PROMISED ABRAHAM HE WOULD GIVE HIM A SON, A PEOPLE AND A LAND.

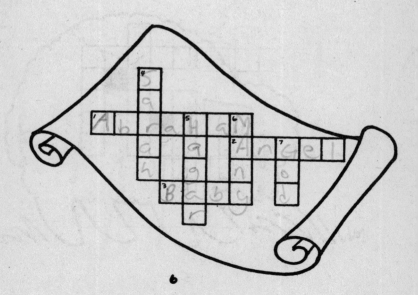

ISHMAEL

GENESIS 16-21

ACROSS

1) HAGAR & ISHMAEL BECAME LOST IN THE _____.
2) ISHMAEL BECAME A SKILLED _____ WHEN HE WAS GROWN.
3) OPPOSITE OF SHORT.
4) BOW AND _____.

DOWN

5) ABRAHAM WAS _____ WHEN HE SENT HAGAR AWAY, UNHAPPY.
6) HAGAR'S SON
7) SARAH'S HANDMAID, ISHMAEL'S MOTHER.

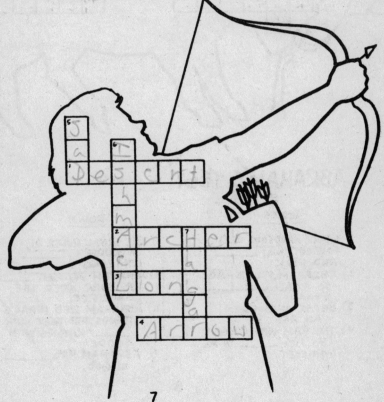

7

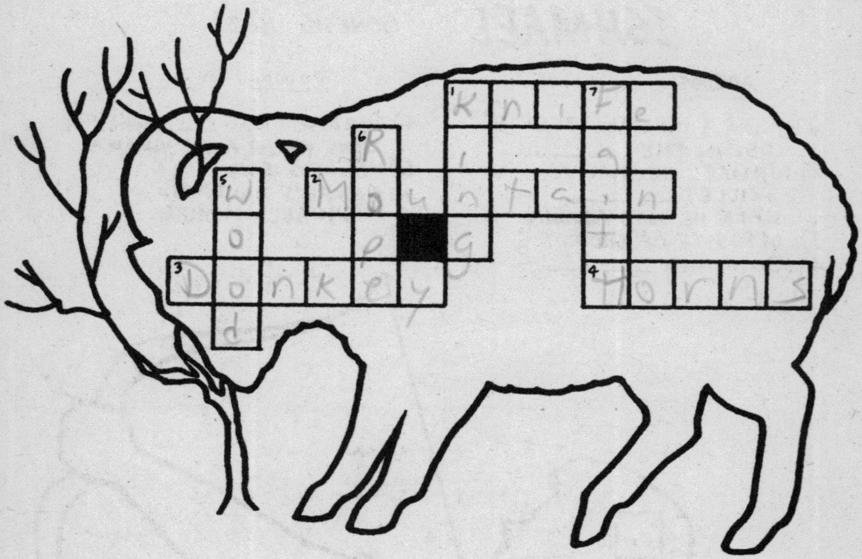

ABRAHAM'S TEST

GENESIS 22:1-13

ACROSS

1) SHARP HANDTOOL USED FOR CUTTING; ______ AND FORK.
2) ABRAHAM TOOK ISAAC TO A TALL ______ PEAK.
3) BEAST OF BURDEN, AN ASS.
4) THE RAM WAS CAUGHT BY HIS ______ IN A THICKET.

DOWN

1) THE ROYAL RULER OF A COUNTRY, "______ OF KINGS".
5) ABRAHAM BROUGHT ______ TO BURN UNDER THE SACRIFICE.
6) ABRAHAM TIED ISAAC'S HANDS AND FEET WITH ______. RHYMES WITH "HOPE".
7) ABRAHAM HAD ______ IN GOD.

JACOB AND ESAU

GENESIS 25:24-34

ACROSS

1) ____ AND ARROW
2) JACOB WAS A ____ MAN, NOT NOISY.
3) ESAU ____ DEER WITH HIS BOW AND ARROW.
4) COVERED WITH LOTS OF HAIR.
5) THE YOUNGER TWIN BORN TO ISAAC AND REBEKAH.
6) JACOB GRABBED ESAU'S ____ AS THEY WERE BORN.

DOWN

1) ESAU SOLD JACOB HIS ____ FOR SOME FOOD.
7) THE OLDER OF THE TWINS.
8) REBEKAH BORE ____ BOYS.
9) JACOB AND ESAU'S MOTHER
10) FIRST AND LAST LETTERS OF THE WORD "USUALLY".

JACOB'S FAMILY

GENESIS 29,30

ACROSS

1) JACOB'S UNCLE
2) JACOB'S FIRST WIFE
3) JACOB HAD HOW MANY SONS?
4) RACHEL LOVED HER HUSBAND, _____.

DOWN

5) JACOB'S SECOND WIFE
6) JACOB'S OLDER TWIN BROTHER
7) JACOB AND RACHEL'S FIRST SON

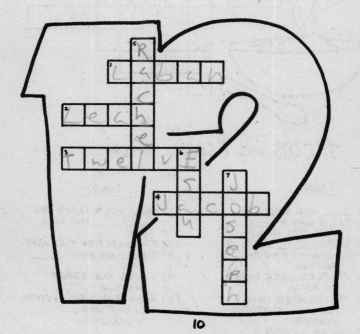

YOUNG JOSEPH

GENESIS 35:16-37

ACROSS

1) JACOB _____ JOSEPH WITH ALL OF HIS HEART.

2) JOSEPH'S FATHER

3) A COAT HAS HOW MANY SLEEVES?

4) JOSEPH HAD HOW MANY OLDER BROTHERS? (THE NUMBER AFTER NINE)

DOWN

5) JOSEPH WAS A YOUNG _____. RHYMES WITH "TOY".

6) JACOB'S YOUNGEST SON

7) "COAT OF MANY _____"

8) JACOB GAVE JOSEPH A SPECIAL, COLORFUL _____.

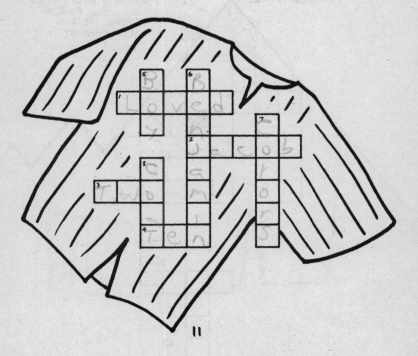

JOSEPH IN EGYPT

GENESIS 39, 40

ACROSS

1) HIGH-RANKING MANSERVANT

2) PHARAOH RULED OVER _____.

3) VISIONS DURING SLEEP

4) GOD WAS _____ JOSEPH.

DOWN

1) ONE WHO BAKES

5) OPPOSITE OF COLD

6) NOT THE TRUTH

7) _____ OF SUNLIGHT; X-_____

8) KING OF EGYPT

9) JOSEPH WAS PUT IN _____ FOR A CRIME HE DID NOT COMMIT.

12

JOSEPH'S BROTHERS VISIT GENESIS 42-44

ACROSS

1) JOSEPH'S YOUNGER BROTHER

2) JOSEPH'S BROTHERS CAME TO BUY _____ TO FEED THEIR FAMILY.

3) AS SECOND IN COMMAND, JOSEPH _____ OVER EGYPT.

DOWN

4) WE USE _____ TO BUY THINGS.

5) A TIME OF NO FOOD, HUNGER

6) JOSEPH'S FATHER

7) OPPOSITE OF WET

8) WHAT NUMBER COMES AFTER NINE?

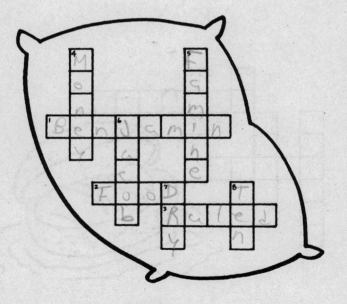

13

BABY MOSES

EXODUS 2:1-10

ACROSS

1) THE DAUGHTER OF A KING IS CALLED A _____.

2) MOSES' _____ WATCHED AS HER BROTHER FLOATED DOWN THE RIVER.

3) MOSES BECAME PHARAOH'S DAUGHTER'S _____.

DOWN

4) MOSES FLOATED DOWN THE RIVER IN A STRAW _____.

5) THE PRINCESS NAMED HER ADOPTED SON _____.

6) OPPOSITE OF DOWN

7) LONG, FLOWING WATERWAY.

14

PLAGUES OF EGYPT

Exodus 7:14 - 10:29

ACROSS

1) THE RIVER WAS TURNED INTO _____.

2) SMALL PARASITIC BUGS RHYMES WITH "NICE"

3) LEAPING AMPHIBIANS

4) OPPOSITE OF LIGHT

5) SWARMS OF GRASSHOPPERS

9) DIRTY, FLYING INSECT PESTS RHYMES WITH "PIES"

DOWN

3) FLAMES

6) RAW SORES ON THE SKIN

7) OPPOSITE OF HEALTHY

8) FROZEN BITS OF ICE FALLING FROM THE SKY DESTROYING CROPS

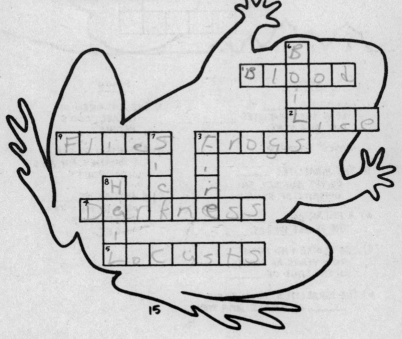

15

THE EXODUS

EXODUS 13:17-22

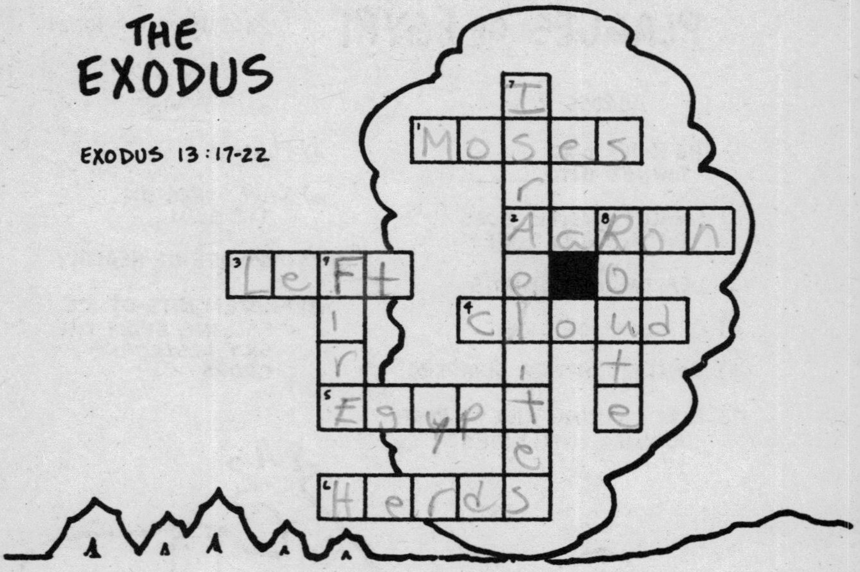

Moses
Aaron
Left
Cloud
Egypt
Herds
Israelite
Route
Fire

ACROSS

1) GOD CHOSE _____ TO LEAD THE ISRAELITES OUT OF EGYPT.

2) MOSES' BROTHER

3) THE ISRAELITES _____ EGYPT QUICKLY. THE OPPOSITE OF STAYED.

4) A PILLAR OF _____ LED THE PEOPLE BY DAY.

5) THE PEOPLE HAD SPENT 400 YEARS AS SLAVES IN THE LAND OF _____.

6) THE ISRAELITES TOOK THEIR _____ OF CATTLE WITH THEM.

DOWN

7) THE CHILDREN OF ISRAEL, GOD'S PEOPLE

8) A CERTAIN COURSE OF A JOURNEY. RHYMES WITH "POUT"

9) A PILLAR OF _____ WAS WITH THE PEOPLE AT NIGHT.

MANNA

EXODUS 16

DOWN

2) THE ISRAELITES COULD _____ THE MANNA INTO BREAD.
3) EACH _____ THE PEOPLE HAD MANNA TO EAT.
4) GROUND BIRDS GOD PROVIDED FOR MEAT
5) GOD GAVE THE PEOPLE ENOUGH _____ TO DRINK.

ACROSS

1) FOOD THAT FELL FROM HEAVEN FROM GOD
2) TO COOK SOMETHING IN BUBBLING HOT WATER
3) A BARREN, DRY LAND

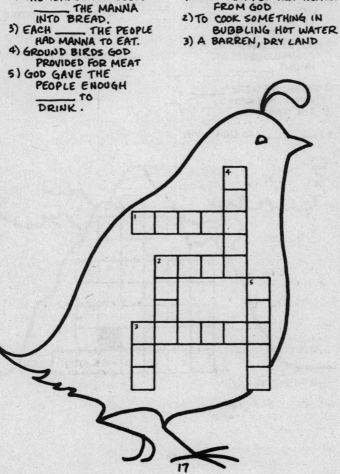

MOSES ON MT. SINAI

EXODUS 19

ACROSS

1) MOSES CLIMBED ALL THE
   WAY TO THE _____
   OF MT. SINAI.

2) MOSES RECEIVED THE 10
   COMMANDMENTS ON
   MOUNT _____.

3) THE PEOPLE WERE _____
   WHEN THEY HEARD
   THE THUNDER.

4) _____ AND LIGHTNING

DOWN

2) OPPOSITE OF STOP-
   RHYMES WITH "PART"

5) A TALL PEAK OF LAND

6) A FEMALE DEER

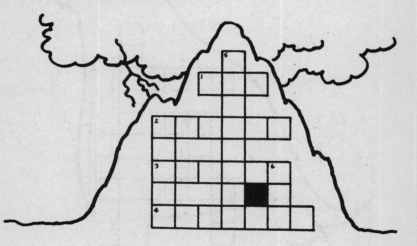

THE GOLDEN CALF

EXODUS 32

ACROSS

1) MOSES' BROTHER WHO MADE THE GOLDEN CALF

2) A FALSE GOD

3) MOSES _____ THE STONE TABLETS WHEN HE SAW THE PEOPLE WORSHIPING THE GOLDEN CALF. (RHYMES WITH "CROAK")

DOWN

4) TO BREAK GOD'S LAW IS _____.

5) A BABY COW

6) THE PEOPLE'S SIN MADE GOD _____. (MAD)

7) THE _____ CALF

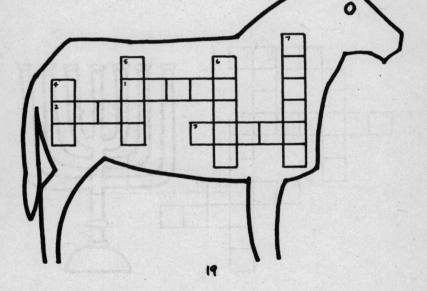

19

THE PRIESTS   EXODUS 28

ACROSS

1) ONLY A PRIEST COULD ENTER THE _____ PLACE.

2) GOD SAID NOT TO _____ IDOLS

3) THE PRIESTS WERE BAREFOOT, NOTHING ON THEIR _____.

4) GOD CHOSE AARON AND HIS _____ TO BE THE PRIESTS.

DOWN

5) MOSES' BROTHER, HIGH PRIEST

6) ONLY MEN FROM THE TRIBE OF _____ COULD BE PRIESTS

7) AARON AND HIS SONS WERE _____.

8) OPPOSITE OF FROM- RHYMES WITH "DO"

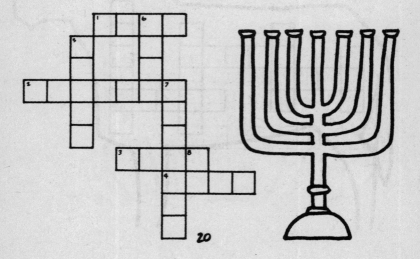

20

BALAAM

ACROSS

1) BALAAM ____ HIS DONKEY WITH A STICK.

2) AN _____ OF GOD STOOD IN BALAAM'S WAY.

3) BALAAM'S _____ COULD SEE THE ANGEL. (AN ASS)

4) THE ANGEL HELD A SHARP _____.

DOWN

5) ____ DID NOT WANT BALAAM TO CURSE HIS CHOSEN PEOPLE (THE LORD).

6) THE DONKEY _____ TO BALAAM! (RHYMES WITH "WALKED")

7) THE DONKEY CRUSHED BALAAM'S FOOT AGAINST A _____. (RHYMES WITH "BALL")

21

CROSSING THE JORDAN

JOSHUA 3

ACROSS

1) THE _____ OF THE COVENANT

2) THE NATION OF ISRAEL HAD HOW MANY TRIBES?

3) THE PEOPLE CROSSED THE JORDAN RIVER ON _____ LAND.

4) ROCKS

DOWN

5) THE LEVITE _____ CARRIED THE ARK OF THE COVENANT.

6) THE _____ IN THE RIVER JORDAN PARTED TO ALLOW THE PEOPLE TO PASS ON DRY LAND.

7) THE PRIESTS AND ARK _____ THE PEOPLE ACROSS THE RIVER FIRST (RHYMES WITH BED)

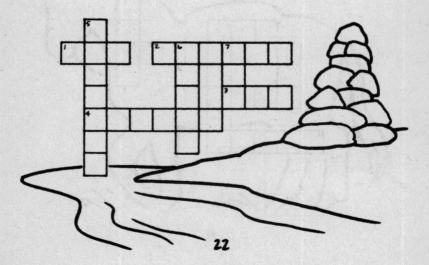

22

THE WALLS OF JERICHO FALL

JOSHUA 6

ACROSS

1) THE PEOPLE MARCHED _____ THE CITY.

2) THE TRUMPETS WERE MADE FROM _____ HORNS. (MALE SHEEP)

3) THE WALLS OF THIS CITY FELL.

4) AS PROMISED, RAHAB'S FAMILY WAS KEPT ____ THROUGH THE BATTLE.

5) THE PEOPLE'S SHOUT MADE THE _____ OF JERICHO FALL.

DOWN

6) THE PRIESTS BLEW THESE INSTRUMENTS.

7) THE PEOPLE DID _____ WITH A LOUD VOICE.

8) AS GOD SAID THEY WOULD, THE WALLS OF JERICHO _____.

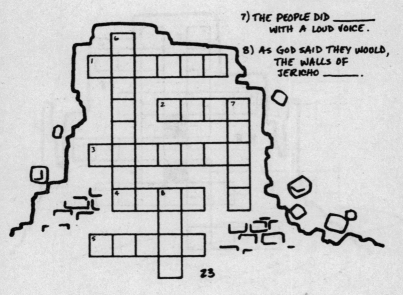

23

CALEB'S VICTORY

ACROSS

1) CALEB WAS NOT YOUNG.
   HE WAS _____.

2) CALEB WAS NOT WEAK,
   BUT VERY_____.

3) _____ LED HIS ARMY
   TO VICTORY OVER THE
   CITY OF HEBRON.

4) HUGE, TALL PEOPLE

5) A GROUP OF SOLDIERS
   UNDER THE SAME
   COMMAND

DOWN

6) CALEB WAS 85
   _____ OLD.

7) TALL PEAK OF LAND

8) A LARGE TOWN -
   RHYMES WITH
   "PRETTY"

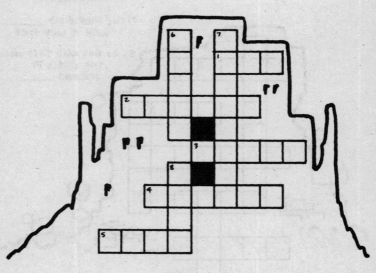

24

JOSHUA'S WORDS

JOSHUA 23, 24

ACROSS

1) JOSHUA WARNED THE PEOPLE NOT TO _____ THEIR PROMISE TO GOD.

2) THE PEOPLE PROMISED THAT THEY WOULD SERVE THE _____.

3) " _____ AND ORDER "

DOWN

4) JOSHUA SET UP A HUGE _____ AS A MONUMENT. (ROCK)

5) OPPOSITE OF NONE

6) JOSHUA WROTE DOWN THE PEOPLE'S PROMISE IN THE _____ OF THE LAW.

7) JOSHUA SAID, "DON'T WORSHIP _____." (FALSE GODS)

25

DEBORAH THE JUDGE

ACROSS

1) DEBORAH WAS A _____ OVER ISRAEL (RHYMES WITH "NUDGE").

2) SHE WOULD _____ UNDER A PALM TREE.

3) THE ONLY WOMAN JUDGE TO RULE OVER THE ISRAELITES.

4) IF YOU ARE WISE, YOU ARE FULL OF _____. (GOOD JUDGEMENT)

DOWN

5) DEBORAH GAVE GOOD _____ TO THOSE WHO CAME TO HER SEEKING COUNSEL (ENDS WITH "ICE").

6) OPPOSITE OF BAD

7) DEBORAH SAT UNDER A _____ TREE. (RHYMES WITH "CALM")

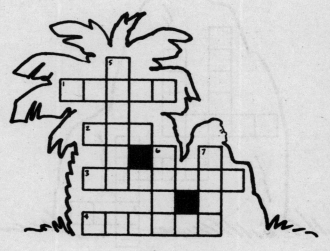

GIDEON'S VICTORY

ACROSS

1) USED FOR LIGHT IN THE DARKNESS (RHYMES WITH CAMP)

2) GIDEON'S SOLDIERS BLEW THEIR _____.

7) A BIRD HATCHES FROM AN _____.

DOWN

3) GIDEON'S 300 MEN DEFEATED THE MIGHTY MIDIANITE _____ IN BATTLE.

4) A CONTAINER FOR HOLDING AND POURING WATER

5) BRAVERY

6) GIDEON'S VICTORY WAS WON WITH ONLY 300 STRONG _____.

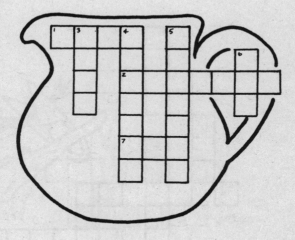

SAMSON & DELILAH

JUDGES 15,16

ACROSS

1) SAMSON WAS VERY
   _____, NOT WEAK.

2) THE WOMAN WHO LEARNED
   THE SOURCE OF SAMSON'S
   STRENGTH, THEN
   BETRAYED HIM

3) LARGE, VERTICAL COLUMNS
   IN A BUILDING, RHYMES
   WITH "FILLERS"

DOWN

4) THE KING OF BEASTS,
   SAMSON KILLED ONE

5) SAMSON DESTROYED THE
   PHILISTINE _____
   BY KNOCKING DOWN
   ITS PILLARS.

6) NOT ABLE TO SEE

7) DELILAH CUT SAMSON'S
   _____ DESTROYING
   HIS STRENGTH.

28

HANNAH'S PROMISE   1 SAMUEL 1

ACROSS

1) GOD ANSWERED HANNAH'S PRAYER FOR A _____ BOY.

2) HANNAH WAS SAD BECAUSE SHE HAD NO _____. (KIDS)

3) TO TALK TO GOD

9) SMALL DRINKING CONTAINERS RHYMES WITH "PUPS"

DOWN

4) HANNAH'S SON

5) OPPOSITE OF NO

6) OPPOSITE OF HE

7) GOD _____ HIS PROMISES.

8) WEEP

29

GOD CALLS SAMUEL

I SAMUEL 3:1-18

ACROSS

1) TO QUESTION, RHYMES WITH "TASK"

2) WHAT WE DO AT NIGHT WHEN WE'RE TIRED

3) THE PRIEST WHO CARED FOR SAMUEL

4) WE SLEEP IN A _____.

5) OPPOSITE OF STOP

DOWN

4) OPPOSITE OF GIRL

6) SAMUEL HEARD GOD CALL HIS _____ FOUR TIMES

7) GOD _____ SAMUEL BY NAME THAT NIGHT. (RHYMES WITH "WALLED")

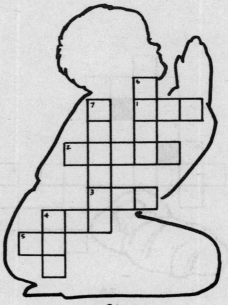

SAMUEL PRAYS FOR VICTORY

I SAMUEL 7:1-14

ACROSS

1) VIOLENT WEATHER DISTURBANCE — RHYMES WITH "FORM"

2) OPPOSITE OF YES

3) OPPOSITE OF GOOD

4) THE PHILISTINES WERE AFRAID AND _____ AWAY.

DOWN

3) THE PHILISTINES FLED AND NEVER CAME _____.

5) TO TALK TO GOD

6) _____ AND LIGHTNING

7) WITH GOD'S HELP, THE ISRAELITES _____ THE BATTLE. (VICTORY)

31

SAUL'S MISTAKES

1 SAMUEL 13,14

ACROSS

1) A GROUP OF SOLDIERS

2) A SWEET SYRUP BEES MAKE

3) SAUL COMMANDED HIS ARMY NOT TO _____ ANY FOOD FOR A DAY.

4) SAUL'S SOLDIERS WERE WEAK AND _____ FROM FIGHTING AND NOT EATING. (RHYMES WITH "FIRED")

DOWN

5) ONLY A _____ WAS ALLOWED TO OFFER SACRIFICES OR GO INTO THE HOLY OF HOLIES.

6) A STAND OF MANY TREES

7) A PERSON _____ TO EAT FOOD TO HAVE ENERGY. (RHYMES WITH "SEEDS")

DAVID FIGHTS GOLIATH   1 SAMUEL 17

ACROSS

1) THE SPIRIT OF _____ WAS WITH DAVID.

2) HOW MANY STONES DID DAVID CHOOSE FOR HIS SLING? (THE NUMBER AFTER FOUR)

3) A PIECE OF ARMOR (RHYMES WITH "FIELD")

4) THE PHILISTINE GIANT

5) GOLIATH WAS NINE FEET _____.

6) THE FIRST WOMAN GOD CREATED

DOWN

3) DAVID'S WEAPON

7) "_____ AND GOLIATH"

8) GOD WAS _____ DAVID

9) DAVID _____ GOLIATH WITH HIS OWN SWORD. (SLEW)

10) DAVID HURLED A _____ AT THE GIANTS FOREHEAD.

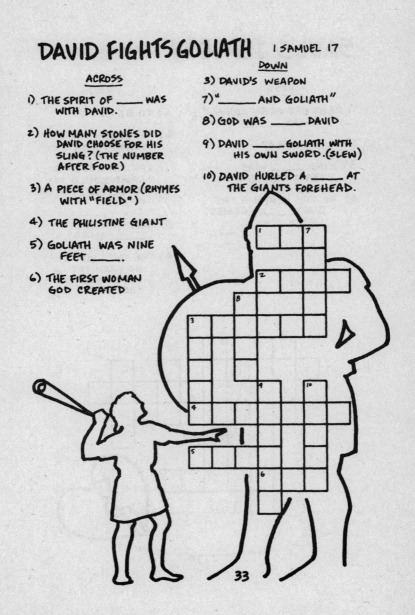

33

SAUL'S JEALOSY

1 SAMUEL 18:5-16

ACROSS

1) DAVID HAD GREAT COURAGE, HE WAS _____.

2) TO HAVE FEAR

3) KING _____ WAS JEALOUS OF DAVID.

4) IN THE MORNING THE SUN _____. (COMES UP)

DOWN

5) TO BE ENVIOUS

6) ATTEMPT- RHYMES WITH "CRY"

7) SAUL WAS AFRAID DAVID WOULD TRY TO BE _____ INSTEAD OF HIM.

8) SAUL WAS OFTEN _____. (MAD)

9) THE TWO LIMBS THAT GO FROM THE SHOULDERS TO THE HANDS

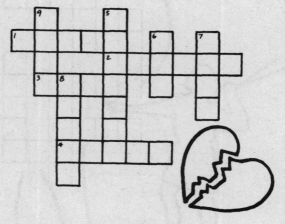

DAVID HIDES
I SAMUEL 21,22

ACROSS

1) OPPOSITE OF IN

2) THE PRIEST GAVE DAVID LOAVES OF _____.

3) DAVID'S ARMY HAD 400 BRAVE _____.

4) WITHOUT FOOD DAVID BECAME _____.

DOWN

5) THE GIANT WHO DAVID SLEW

6) BATH _____ (RHYMES WITH "RUB")

7) DAVID HID IN A _____. (RHYMES WITH "SAVE")

8) A GROUP OF SOLDIERS

9) JEWELRY YOU WEAR ON A FINGER.

10) LONG, SHARP, BLADED WEAPON

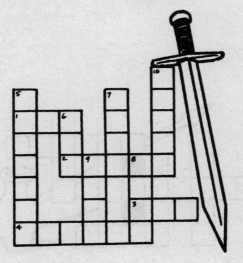

SAUL LIVES

I SAMUEL 26

ACROSS

1) KING SAUL WAS
   _____ ONE NIGHT,
   NOT AWAKE.

2) OPPOSITE OF
   INSIDE

3) WE HEAR WITH
   OUR _____.

DOWN

4) DAVID STOLE SAUL'S
   BOTTLE OF
   _____.

5) OPPOSITE OF DIE

6) VERY LONG WEAPON
   WITH A POINT
   ON THE END

7) YOU WEAR A HAT
   ON IT

SAUL DIES

I SAMUEL 31

ACROSS

1) ROYAL MEN WHO RULE
   OVER COUNTRIES
   (RHYMES WITH "SINGS")

2) SAUL'S BOYS, HIS _____,
   DIED IN BATTLE.

3) SAUL FELL ON HIS OWN
   SWORD AND _____.

DOWN

4) SAUL _____ GREATLY
   AGAINST GOD WHEN
   HE WENT TO THE
   FORTUNE TELLER.

5) LONG, SHARP, BLADED
   WEAPON

6) ISRAEL WAS DEFEATED
   AND _____ THE
   BATTLE AGAINST THE
   PHILISTINES.

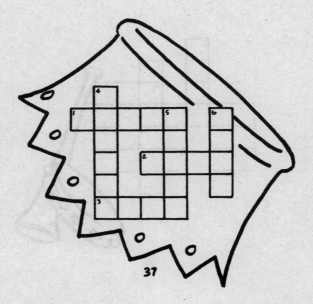

37

DAVID AND THE ARK

2 SAMUEL 6

ACROSS

1) STRONG CATTLE THAT PULLED THE WAGON

2) _____ OF THE COVENANT

3) LARGE, WHEELED CART PULLED BY OXEN

4) TEMPORARY DWELLING MADE OF HIDES OR FABRIC

DOWN

3) AN OWL ASKS, "_____?"

5) THE PEOPLE SANG A JOYFUL _____.

6) KING DAVID _____ WITH JOY (RHYMES WITH "LANCED").

7) GOD _____ HIS PROMISE.

38

DAVID'S SIN

2 SAMUEL 11

ACROSS

1) OPPOSITE OF GOOD

2) DAVID FELL IN _____ WITH BATHSHEBA.

3) OPPOSITE OF SUNRISE.

4) BATHSHEBA WAS ALREADY MARRIED TO ANOTHER _____.

DOWN

1) BEAUTIFUL MEANS FULL OF _____.

5) THE TOP OF A BUILDING

6) OPPOSITE OF OFF

7) TO BREAK GOD'S LAW — RHYMES WITH "PIN"

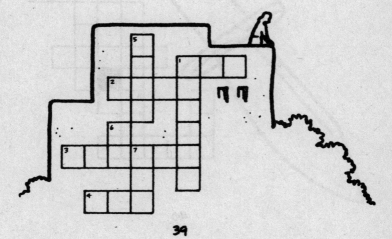

DAVID'S TROUBLED SONS 2 SAMUEL 13

ACROSS

1) TO TAKE A LIFE

2) DAVID STILL _____ HIS WICKED SON WITH ALL HIS HEART.

3) OPPOSITE OF SHE

4) PERIODS OF 365 DAYS – RHYMES WITH "FEARS"

DOWN

5) BAD, EVIL

6) DAVID'S SON KILLED HIS OWN _____. (RHYMES WITH "MOTHER")

7) TO WEEP

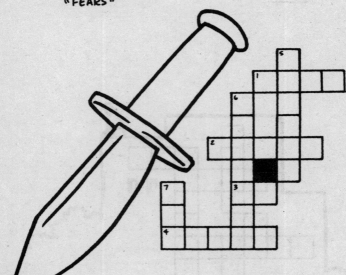

DAVID'S LOYAL FRIENDS

2 SAMUEL 16,15

ACROSS

1) DAVID'S FRIENDS SAVED HIS _____.

2) ASSISTANCE - RHYMES WITH "KELP"

3) OPPOSITE OF BAD

4) PEOPLE SLEEP IN _____.

DOWN

5) PEOPLE WHO LIKE EACH OTHER ARE _____ (RHYMES WITH "ENDS").

6) OPPOSITE OF BOTTOM

7) DAVID'S FRIENDS BROUGHT _____ FOR HIM TO EAT. (RHYMES WITH "RUDE")

41

DAVID, KING AGAIN

2 SAMUEL 19

ACROSS

1) WHAT A KING WEARS
   ON HIS HEAD

2) HOW OLD A PERSON IS
   IS THEIR _____.
   (RHYMES WITH "PAGE")

3) NO WARS OR FIGHTING
   GOING ON

DOWN

4) THE SPECIAL CHAIR
   A KING SITS ON

5) DAVID WAS MADE _____
   OVER ISRAEL AGAIN.
   (RHYMES WITH "SING")

6) TO CLEAN SOMETHING
   WITH WATER, SUCH
   AS, _____ DISHES

7) OPPOSITE OF HAPPY

42

YOUNG SOLOMON ANOINTED 1 KINGS 1:38-53

ACROSS

1) DAVID WAS GETTING ____, NOT YOUNG.

2) DAVID'S SON, _____, WOULD BE ISRAEL'S NEW KING.

3) ZADOK, A _____, ANOINTED SOLOMON (RHYMES WITH "LEAST").

DOWN

1) SOLOMON WAS ANOINTED WITH ____.

2) SOLOMON WAS DAVID'S ____.

4) SOLOMON RODE ON DAVID'S ____, A CROSS BETWEEN A HORSE AND A DONKEY. (RHYMES WITH "RULE")

5) SOLOMON WOULD BE THE _____ KING AFTER KING DAVID (RHYMES WITH "TEXT").

6) SOLOMON _____ ON HIS FATHER'S MULE.

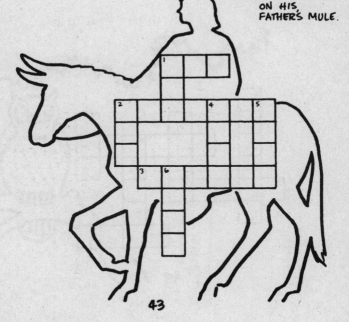

43

SOLOMON'S WISDOM

1 KINGS 3: 5-15
1 KINGS 4: 29-34

ACROSS

1) MUCH WEALTH

2) SOLOMON WANTED TO _____ GOD (RHYMES WITH "CURVE").

3) TO TALK TO GOD

DOWN

4) OPPOSITE OF QUESTION

5) SOLOMON WAS VERY _____. HE HAD GREAT WISDOM.

6) "_____THY MOTHER AND THY FATHER."

7) TO QUESTION— RHYMES WITH "TASK"

44

THE TEMPLE

I KINGS 5:1-9
9:1-7

ACROSS

1) STEPS GOING UP
AND DOWN

2) PEOPLE _____ UP
THE TEMPLE STEPS
TO GO TO WORSHIP
(RHYMES WITH "TALKED")

3) THE KIND OF WOOD
THEY USED TO BUILD
THE TEMPLE - RHYMES
WITH "FEEDER"

4) SET APART TO GOD -
_____ OF HOLIES

DOWN

1) A TWINKLING LIGHT
IN THE NIGHT SKY

2) LARGE, FLAT SIDES
OF A ROOM OR
BUILDING

5) SOLOMON BUILT THE
_____.

6) THE _____ OF THE
COVENANT WAS
PLACED IN THE
TEMPLE.

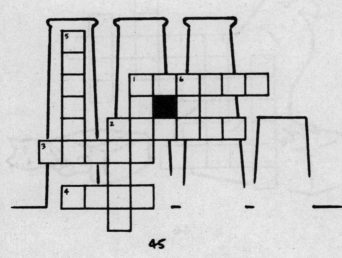

45

SOLOMON'S SINS

2 KINGS 11

ACROSS

1) KING OF EGYPT

2) FALSE GODS

3) SOLOMON MARRIED
   THE PHARAOH'S
   DAUGHTER WHO
   WAS FROM _____.

DOWN

1) OPPOSITE OF RICH

4) EVIL, BAD

5) SOLOMON MADE LIFE
   _____ (DIFFICULT)
   FOR THE POOR PEOPLE.
   (RHYMES WITH "CARD")

6) PRECIOUS YELLOW METAL

7) OPPOSITE OF DOWN

ELIJAH

1 KINGS 17

ACROSS

1) LARGE BLACK BIRDS LIKE CROWS - RHYMES WITH "HAVENS"

2) WATER THAT FALLS FROM THE SKY

3) ELIJAH HAD A LONG, SCRUFFY _____ GROWING FROM HIS CHIN.

DOWN

4) ELIJAH'S _____ WAS GROWN OUT LONG (RHYMES WITH "CHAIR").

5) _____ WAS A PROPHET OF GOD WITH LONG HAIR AND BEARD.

6) ELIJAH WORE CLOTHES MADE FROM ANIMAL _____, NOT CLOTH.

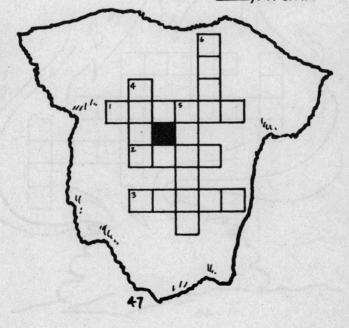

ELIJAH'S CHALLENGE

I KINGS 18:17-40

ACROSS

1) NOT TRUE

2) HEAVY, BIG CATTLE

3) FLAMES

4) ELIJAH OFFERED HIS SACRIFICE ON AN _____.

DOWN

5) FALSE GOD

6) WATER THAT FALLS FROM THE SKY

7) GOD'S PROPHET WHO THE RAVENS FED

8) OPPOSITE OF TO

48

ELISHA JOINS ELIJAH

1 KINGS 19:19-21

ACROSS

1) BIG, STRONG CATTLE USED FOR PULLING PLOWS

2) ELISHA WAS WORKING THE _____ OF HIS FAMILY'S FARM (RHYMES WITH "SHIELDS").

3) MOTHER AND FATHER

DOWN

4) ELIJAH PUT HIS CLOAK OF ANIMAL _____ ONTO ELISHA.

5) WHERE FOOD IS GROWN "OLD MACDONALD'S _____ "

6) OPPOSITE OF HELLO

7) _____ JOINED ELIJAH TO BE A PROPHET.

ELIJAH TAKEN UP INTO HEAVEN

2 KINGS 2:1-11

ACROSS

1) _____ PULL CHARIOTS.
(RHYMES WITH "FORCES")

2) TWO-WHEELED BATTLE
WAGON PULLED
BY HORSES

3) FLAMES

4) MOVEMENT OF AIR —
RHYMES WITH "PINNED"

DOWN

1) GOD'S DWELLING PLACE
ON HIGH

5) OPPOSITE OF ON

6) OPPOSITE OF OUT

7) TO CONSUME FOOD

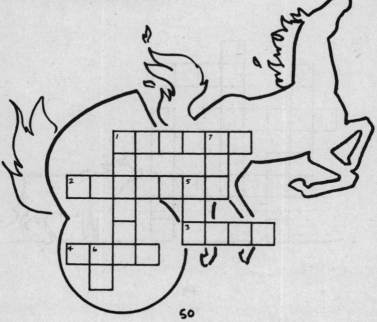

ELISHA AND THE OIL

2 KINGS 4:1-7

ACROSS

1) OPPOSITE OF DOWN

2) THE WIDOW COULD NOW _____ OFF THE DEBT (RHYMES WITH "HAY").

3) TALL CONTAINERS FOR LIQUID - RHYMES WITH "THROTTLES"

4) THE WIDOW _____ ALL OF THE JARS TO THEIR TOPS.

DOWN

5) LAMPS BURN _____ FOR LIGHT

6) WE USE THIS TO BUY THINGS.

7) LARGE MOUTH CONTAINERS - RHYMES WITH "LOTS"

8) CONTAINERS WITH LIDS - RHYMES WITH "CARS"

9) " _____ AND EVERY ONE " RHYMES WITH "PEACH"

PEOPLE HEALED
FROM POISON

2 KINGS 4:38-41

ACROSS

1) OPPOSITE OF LOSE -
   RHYMES WITH "KIND"

2) A TOXIC, DEADLY
   SUBSTANCE USUALLY
   IN DRINK OR FOOD

3) TO CONSUME FOOD

DOWN

1) WE EAT ____ TO
   STAY ALIVE

2) THEY COOKED THE
   STEW IN A BIG
   ____ (RHYMES
   WITH "LOT").

4) ILL

5) OPPOSITE OF OUT

52

NAAMAN HEALED 2 KINGS 5

ACROSS

1) THE OUTER COVERING OF OUR BODIES - RHYMES WITH "SPIN"

2) TO CLEAN WITH WATER, SUCH AS ____DISHES

3) SOMEONE WITH LEPROSY - RHYMES WITH "PEPPER"

4) THE NUMBER THAT COMES AFTER SIX

DOWN

1) A STRONG BOX TO LOCK VALUABLES IN

5) TO HAVE A DISEASE CURED

6) OPPOSITE OF FUTURE

7) _____ WAS HEALED OF HIS LEPROSY

8) A LONG, FLOWING BODY OF WATER

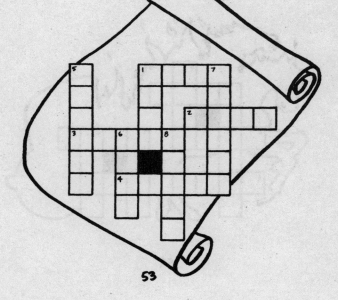

ELISHA AND THE CHARIOTS OF FIRE

2 KINGS 6:8-23

ACROSS

1) WE HEAR WITH OUR _____.

2) A LARGE TOWN

3) FLAMES

4) 2-WHEELED WAR WAGONS PULLED BY SWIFT HORSES

DOWN

1) GOD SAVED THE PROPHET _____ BY SENDING FIERY CHARIOTS.

3) WE EAT _____ TO LIVE.

5) A GROUP OF SOLDIERS

6) IF YOU'RE TIRED, YOU SHOULD TAKE A _____ (RHYMES WITH "BEST")

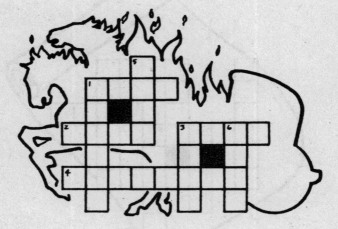

56

ELISHA DIES

2 KINGS 13:14-21

ACROSS

1) OPPOSITE OF SMALL

2) TWO-WHEELED WAR WAGON PULLED BY SWIFT HORSES

3) THE NUMBER AFTER THE NUMBER TWO

DOWN

1) _____ AND ARROW

4) A BOW SHOOTS _____.

5) TO STRIKE SOMETHING - RHYMES WITH "FIT"

6) GOD'S PROPHET WHO JOINED ELIJAH

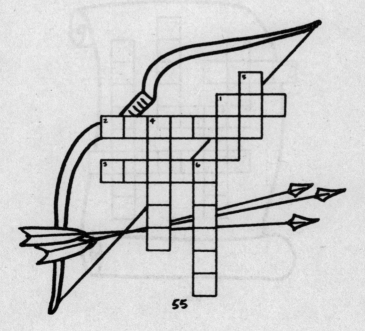

55

HEZEKIAH

2 KINGS 18

ACROSS

1) OPPOSITE OF BAD

2) A QUEEN'S HUSBAND-
   RHYMES WITH
   "RING"

3) KING HEZEKIAH
   WOULD ONLY
   _____ THE
   ONE TRUE
   GOD.

DOWN

4) OPPOSITE OF OLD

5) KING _____
   LOVED GOD AND
   DESTROYED
   THE IDOLS.

6) FALSE GODS

7) MANY PAGES BOUND
   TOGETHER IS A
   _____ (RHYMES
   WITH "COOK").

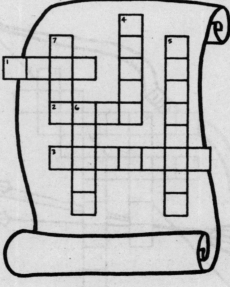

56

HEZEKIAH'S MISTAKE   2 KINGS 20:12-19

ACROSS

1) PRECIOUS WHITE METAL - FORKS AND SPOONS ARE _____WARE.

2) A PAPER SHOWING ROADS, CITIES ETC. ON IT - RHYMES WITH "TAP"

3) OPPOSITE OF POOR

4) KEPT FROM THE KNOWLEDGE OF OTHERS, UNREVEALED, HIDDEN

DOWN

1) SEASONINGS "SUGAR AND _____"

5) HARD, PROTECTIVE SUIT WORN BY SOLDIERS

6) PRECIOUS YELLOW METAL

7) RICHES, VALUABLES; "_____ CHEST" RHYMES WITH "MEASURE"

JOSIAH, THE YOUNG KING

2 KINGS 22

ACROSS

1) GOD SAID TO _____ HIS LAW
   (RHYMES WITH "SHEEP").
2) MANY PAGES BOUND TOGETHER
   ARE A _____.
3) PERIODS OF 365 DAYS
4) OPPOSITE OF LOST

DOWN

5) OPPOSITE OF SHE
6) HUMAN BEINGS, A
   NATION, A RACE -
   RHYMES WITH "STEEPLE"
7) OPPOSITE OF HAPPY

58

GOD FIGHTS FOR JEHOSHAPHAT'S ARMY

2 CHRONICLES
20:22-30

ACROSS

1) ASSISTANCE - RHYMES WITH "KELP"
2) BLACK, GOOEY SUBSTANCE USED ON ROADS - RHYMES WITH "CAR"
3) JEHOSHAPHAT PRAYED AND GOD HEARD ____ (RHYMES WITH "DIM").
4) GOD DESTROYED JUDAH'S ____ (ADVERSARY, FOE).
5) JUDAH WAS ____ BY THE LORD (RHYMES WITH "PAVED".

DOWN

6) PRIESTS CAME FROM THE TRIBE OF ____.
7) JUDAH'S ENEMIES FOUGHT EACH ____.
8) YOU MUST TAKE ____ AT A TARGET BEFORE YOU SHOOT IT.
9) A GROUP OF SOLDIERS
10) NO WAR OR FIGHTING - RHYMES WITH "NIECE"

KING UZZIAH

2 CHRONICLES 26:1-15

ACROSS

1) _____ BECAME KING WHEN HE WAS 16.

2) THE NUMBER THAT COMES AFTER FIFTEEN

3) TALL, NARROW BUILDINGS - RHYMES WITH "FLOWERS"

4) OPPOSITE OF MORE

5) " _____ LIKE AN EAGLE". RHYMES WITH "POOR"

6) OPPOSITE OF FEW

DOWN

7) FARMS THAT GROW GRAPES

8) DEEP HOLES IN THE GROUND FOR WATER

9) OPPOSITE OF WEAK

10) FEMALE CHICKEN

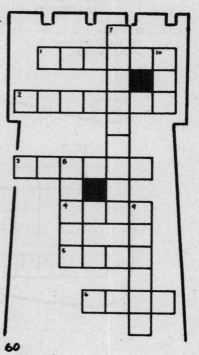

THE PEOPLE RETURN

EZRA 2:1 - 3:7

ACROSS

1) SACRIFICES WERE
   OFFERED ON
   AN _____.

2) OPPOSITE OF OVER

3) TO GO BACK TO THE
   PLACE YOU
   CAME FROM

4) THE PEOPLE SANG
   _____ OF JOY
   WHEN THEY WERE
   SET FREE TO
   GO HOME.

DOWN

5) OPPOSITE OF FIRST

6) BROKEN DOWN,
   ABANDONED CITY
   OR BUILDING -
   THE GREEK
   PARTHENON
   IS IN _____.

7) OPPOSITE OF UP

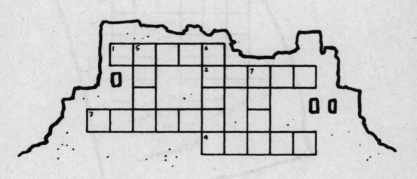

61

THE BUILDING STOPS

EZRA 4

ACROSS

1) A WRITTEN COMMUNICATION - RHYMES WITH "BETTER"

2) OPPOSITE OF START

3) AN INSTRUMENT USED TO WRITE, USES INK

DOWN

1) OPPOSITE OF FOUND

4) HOUSE OF WORSHIP

5) ONE WHO RULES - RHYMES WITH "COOLER"

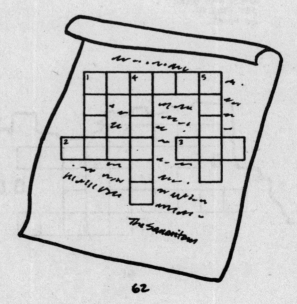

EZRA

EZRA 7

ACROSS

1) TO TALK, TO UTTER WORDS

2) ONE WHO SPEAKS FOR GOD

3) "_____ OF A NEEDLE"

DOWN

1) ONE WHO COPIED BOOKS AND DID THE JOB OF WRITING THINGS DOWN - RHYMES WITH "BRIBE"

4) TO GIVE INSTRUCTION, TO CAUSE TO LEARN, TO EDUCATE

5) ONLY THE _____ COULD GO INTO THE HOLY TABERNACLE

6) _____ WAS A PRIEST, PROPHET AND SCRIBE.

NEHEMIAH PRAYS

NEHEMIAH 1

ACROSS

1) OPPOSITE OF ON

2) HEBREWS, CHILDREN OF
   ISRAEL - RHYMES
   WITH "NEWS"

3) OPPOSITE OF GO -
   "O ____, LET US
   ADORE HIM" -
   RHYMES WITH "SOME"

4) TALK TO GOD

DOWN

3) SMALL DRINKING
   CONTAINER - RHYMES
   WITH "PUP"

5) _____ PRAYED TO
   GOD FOR THE CITY
   OF JERUSALEM.

6) OPPOSITE OF SLOW

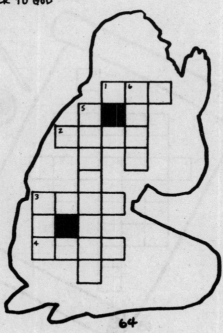

64

THE WALL FINISHED NEHEMIAH 6:15-16

ACROSS

1) TALL, FLAT STRUCTURE SURROUNDING ANCIENT CITIES – RHYMES WITH "CALL"

2) FIX

3) OPPOSITE OF WEAK

4) OPPOSITE OF SHORT

5) THE WHOLE EARTH – RHYMES WITH "CURLED"

DOWN

1) LABOR – RHYMES WITH "PERK"

6) "COME SIT ON MY _____" SAID GRANDMA. (RHYMES WITH "CAP")

7) THE NUMBER THAT FOLLOWS FIFTY-ONE

8) MEN WHO KEEP WATCH OVER SOMEONE OR SOMETHING (RHYMES WITH "YARDS")

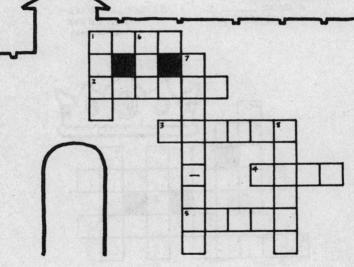

65

ESTHER BECOMES QUEEN

ESTHER 2:1-8

ACROSS

1) OPPOSITE OF OFF

2) FULL OF BEAUTY

3) THE KING OF PERSIA CHOSE _____ TO BE HIS QUEEN.

4) QUEEN ESTHER WORE A ROYAL _____ ON HER HEAD.

DOWN

5) THE KING _____ ESTHER MORE THAN ANY OTHER WOMAN.

6) A KING'S WIFE IS A _____.

7) PRESENTS

8) ONE WHO RULES - A STICK FOR MEASURING

MORDECAI HONORED

ESTHER 6:1-11

ACROSS

1) THE KING OF PERSIA HONORED _____.

2) RESPECT, " _____ THY MOTHER AND THY FATHER "

3) LARGE, SWIFT ANIMAL FOR RIDING - RHYMES WITH "COURSE"

DOWN

1) OPPOSITE OF WOMAN

4) OPPOSITE OF COMMON - RHYMES WITH "CARE"

5) A KING WEARS ONE ON HIS HEAD

6) A MAN _____ ON A HORSE TO RIDE IT (RHYMES WITH "FITS").

67

JOB

JOB

ACROSS

1) OPPOSITE OF RICH

2) HAVING PAIN OR DISTRESS

3) OPPOSITE OF SHE

4) JOB SERVED THE LORD. HE LOVED ____.

DOWN

1) HURT- RHYMES WITH "RAIN"

5) ALOT- RHYMES WITH "SUCH"

6) JOB ____ GOD WITH ALL HIS HEART.

7) GOD TOOK EVERYTHING AWAY FROM HIS SERVANT ____.

8) OPPOSITE OF OUT

9) OPPOSITE OF BAD-JOB WAS A ____ MAN.

68

PSALM 23

ACROSS

1) " I WILL FEAR
   NO _____ "

2) " I WILL DWELL IN THE
   HOUSE OF THE
   LORD _____ "

3) " HE MAKES ME LIE
   DOWN IN _____
   PASTURES "

4) " THE _____ IS MY
   SHEPHERD "

DOWN

3) TO GET BIGGER

5) " THOUGH I WALK
   THROUGH THE _____
   OF THE SHADOW
   OF DEATH "

6) " THE LORD IS MY _____ "

7) " HE LEADS ME BESIDE
   THE _____ WATERS "

8) " SURELY GOODNESS AND
   MERCY SHALL
   FOLLOW _____ "

69

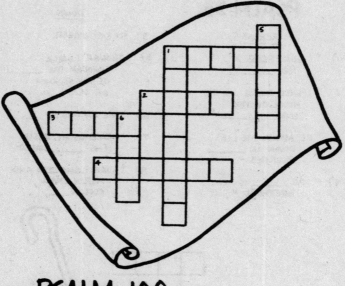

PSALM 100

ACROSS

1) OPPOSITE OF LIE

2) GOD HAS _____ US AND NOT WE OURSELVES (RHYMES WITH "PAID")

3) SING A _____ OF PRAISE

4) FULL OF JOY

DOWN

1) FULL OF THANKS

5) WOOLY CREATURES THAT NEED A SHEPHERD

6) GOD IS _____ (OPPOSITE OF BAD).

PSALM 148

ACROSS

1) "LIGHT HOLDER" OF THE NIGHT SKY

2) SMALL, TWINKLING LIGHTS OF THE NIGHT SKY

3) HUMAN BEINGS, NATION, RACE - RHYMES WITH "STEEPLE"

4) SMALL MOUNTAINS

5) "LIGHT HOLDER" OF THE DAY

6) _____ CREATED EVERYTHING, PRAISE HIM!

DOWN

7) GOD'S MESSENGERS

8) TALL PLANTS WITH TRUNKS - RHYMES WITH "SEAS"

9) WORSHIP, ADORE, EXTOL - RHYMES WITH "RAISE"

10) OPPOSITE OF WOMEN

11) MEN WHO RULE OVER COUNTRIES - RHYMES WITH "RINGS"

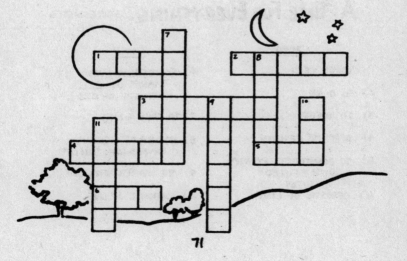

A Time For Everything ECCLESIASTES 3:1-8

ACROSS

1) CLOCKS TELL _____.

2) TO CURE

3) TO WEEP

4) OPPOSITE OF HATE

5) TO CONSTRUCT - RHYMES WITH "FILLED"

6) OPPOSITE OF LOVE

DOWN

4) SOMETHING FUNNY MAKES US _____. (OPPOSITE OF CRY)

7) TO TAKE A LIFE

8) NO WAR OR FIGHTING - RHYMES WITH "NIECE"

9) THE NUMBER AFTER ONE

10) OPPOSITE OF LIVE

ISAIAH'S PROPHESY OF JESUS

ISAIAH 9:6

ACROSS

1) COMING INTO THE WORLD - RHYMES WITH "HORN"

2) ONE WHO COUNSELS

3) OPPOSITE OF LOST

4) VERY YOUNG PERSON, AN OFFSPRING - RHYMES WITH "WILD"

DOWN

5) MARVELOUS, FULL OF WONDER

6) OPPOSITE OF DAUGHTER, "_____ OF GOD"

7) JESUS, THE SON OF _____

8) THE SON OF A KING - RHYMES WITH "SINCE"

JEREMIAH'S VISION

JEREMIAH 24

ACROSS

1) NO WAR OR FIGHTING

2) OPPOSITE OF GOOD

3) SWEET FRUITS OF THE FIG TREE

4) A WRITTEN COMMUNICATION - RHYMES WITH "BETTER"

5) OPPOSITE OF PUSH

DOWN

1) TALK TO GOD

6) PRISONER, HOSTAGE, HELD AGAINST THEIR WILL

7) OPPOSITE OF NONE

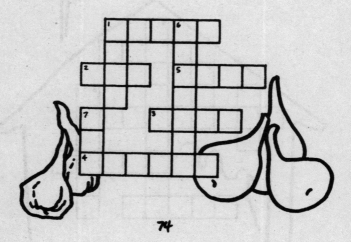

74

ISRAEL IN BABYLON

JEREMIAH 34:1-10
EZEKIEL 37

ACROSS

1) THE CHILDREN OF _____
   WERE TAKEN AWAY
   TO BABYLON.

2) THE JEWS WOULD BE
   CAPTIVES FOR
   SEVENTY _____
   (RHYMES WITH
   "TEARS")

3) TO CONSUME WITH FIRE-
   RHYMES WITH "TURN"

DOWN

4) A LARGE TOWN

5) THE JEWS WERE
   TAKEN TO
   _____.

6) BABYLON WAS A LAND
   FAR _____.

7) THE CHILDREN OF
   ISRAEL WOULD _____
   SONGS TO REMEMBER
   THEIR HOMELAND.

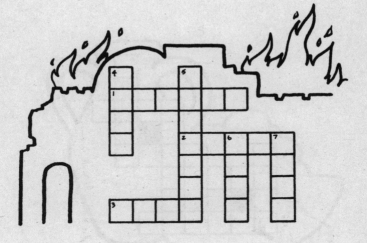

YOUNG DANIEL

DANIEL 1:1-7

ACROSS

1) A SWEET, PURPLE FRUIT - RHYMES WITH "DRUM"

2) A MAN WHO RULES OVER A COUNTRY

3) OPPOSITE OF IN

7) YOUNG _____ WOULD ONLY EAT THE FOOD OF HIS PEOPLE.

DOWN

1) A SON OF A KING

4) OPPOSITE OF OLD

5) DANIEL WOULD NOT EAT THE KING'S _____.

6) THE NUMBER THAT COMES BEFORE ELEVEN

THE FIERY FURNACE

DANIEL 3:19-30

ACROSS

1) TO BE BOUND WITH ROPE — RHYMES WITH "LIED"

2) THICK, LONG CORDS FOR TYING — RHYMES WITH "HOPES"

3) THE NUMBER AFTER THE NUMBER TWO

DOWN

4) KING NEBUCHADNEZZAR WORSHIPED THE ONE TRUE ____ AFTER HE SAW THE MEN COME OUT OF THE FIRE. (OPPOSITE OF FALSE)

5) FLAMES

6) CONSUMED BY FIRE — RHYMES WITH "TURNED"

7) ONE MORE THAN THREE

8) OPPOSITE OF COLD

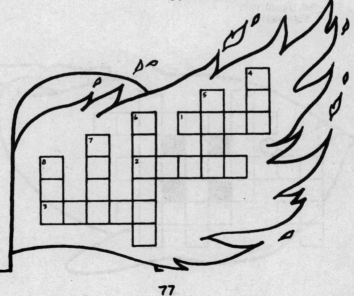

77

JONAH AND THE CITY OF NINEVEH

ACROSS

1) VERY LARGE BODY OF WATER - RHYMES WITH "BEE"

2) FINNED CREATURES OF THE WATER - RHYMES WITH "DISH"

3) TO TAKE FOOD DOWN THE THROAT INTO THE STOMACH - RHYMES WITH "HOLLOW"

4) OPPOSITE OF OUT

5) THE LIQUID THAT FISH SWIM IN

DOWN

3) A LARGE, SEAGOING VESSEL - RHYMES WITH "SLIP"

6) STOMACH - RHYMES WITH "JELLY"

7) JONAH DID NOT WANT TO GO TO THE CITY OF _____.

8) _____ WAS SWALLOWED BY A GREAT FISH.

78

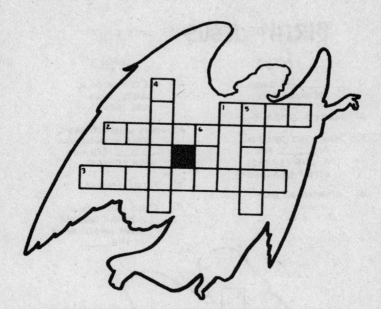

GABRIEL VISITS MARY

LUKE 1:26-38

ACROSS

1) GABRIEL TOLD _____ SHE WOULD BEAR A SON AND CALL HIM JESUS.

2) _____ WOULD BE THE SAVIOR OF THE WORLD.

3) JOSEPH WAS A _____ WHO WORKED WITH WOOD.

DOWN

4) MARY WAS TO BE MARRIED TO _____.

5) A MESSENGER OF GOD, GABRIEL WAS AN _____.

6) OPPOSITE OF DAUGHTER

BIRTH OF JESUS

LUKE 2:1-7

ACROSS

1) _____ WAS BORN IN BETHLEHEM.

2) MARY'S HUSBAND

3) MARY PUT JESUS IN A _____ FOR A CRIB (RHYMES WITH "STRANGER").

4) OPPOSITE OF SHE

DOWN

5) THE CITY OF DAVID, WHERE JESUS WAS BORN

6) MARY WRAPPED BABY JESUS IN SWADDLING _____. (RHYMES WITH "ROSE")

7) JESUS' MOTHER

8) JESUS WAS BORN IN A STABLE BECAUSE THERE WAS NO ROOM AT THE _____.

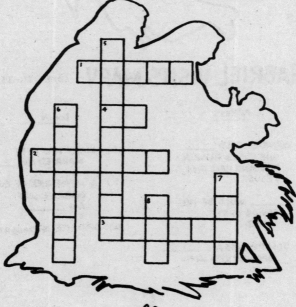

JESUS PRESENTED AT TEMPLE

LUKE 22:21-38

ACROSS

1) HOUSE OF WORSHIP

2) PEACEFUL BIRDS - RHYMES WITH "LOVES"

3) THE NUMBER AFTER THIRTY- NINE

DOWN

4) MARY AND JOSEPH BROUGHT BABY _____ TO THE TEMPLE.

5) FATHER, SON, HOLY _____

6) JESUS IS THE _____ OF THE WORLD (ONE WHO SAVES).

7) THE NUMBER THAT COMES AFTER NUMBER ONE

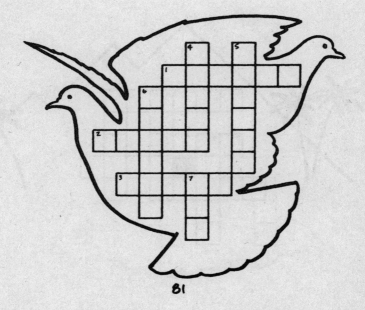

FLIGHT INTO EGYPT

MATTHEW 2:13-18

ACROSS

1) MARY'S HUSBAND

2) VERY YOUNG CHILD -
   RHYMES WITH "MAYBE"

3) SCHEME OR PLAN -
   RHYMES WITH "CLOT"

4) OPPOSITE OF DAY

DOWN

5) THE LAND WHERE
   PHARAOHS ONCE RULED,
   HOME OF THE PYRAMIDS

6) KING _____ SOUGHT
   TO DESTROY BABY
   JESUS.

7) A MESSENGER OF GOD

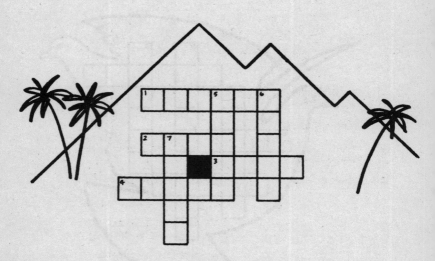

JESUS IN THE TEMPLE

LUKE 2:41-53

ACROSS

1) ONES WHO TEACH, INSTRUCTORS

2) HOUSE OF WORSHIP

3) OPPOSITE OF QUESTIONS

10) MOTHER OF JESUS

DOWN

4) JESUS WAS _____ YEARS OLD (THE NUMBER AFTER ELEVEN)

5) AS A BOY, _____ AMAZED THE TEACHERS IN THE TEMPLE.

6) TO SET UP A TEMPORARY LODGING PLACE - RHYMES WITH "LAMP"

7) ANXIETY, CONCERN, FRET- RHYMES WITH "HURRY"

8) OPPOSITE OF NIGHTS

9) MARY'S HUSBAND

83

JESUS IS BAPTIZED

LUKE 3:21-22

ACROSS

1) _____ THE BAPTIST BAPTIZED JESUS.

2) A BIRD WHICH SYMBOLIZES THE HOLY SPIRIT, PEACE

3) A LONG, FLOWING BODY OF WATER - RHYMES WITH "SLIVER"

4) FATHER, SON, HOLY _____

DOWN

5) OPPOSITE OF OUT

6) "THIS IS MY BELOVED _____ IN WHOM I AM WELL PLEASED" SAID GOD.

7) THEY HEARD GOD'S _____ FROM HEAVEN (RHYMES WITH "CHOICE").

1) THE SON OF GOD

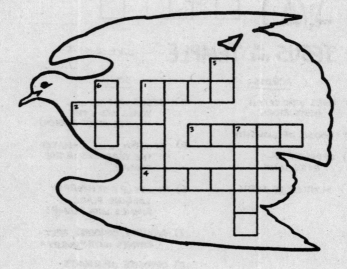

84

ANDREW AND JOHN
JOHN 1:35-39

ACROSS

1) TO GO AFTER SOMEONE -
   RHYMES WITH
   "HOLLOW"

2) A BABY SHEEP

3) SIMON PETER'S
   BROTHER, ONE OF
   CHRIST'S FIRST
   FOLLOWERS

DOWN

4) AUTHOR OF THE FOURTH
   GOSPEL IN THE NEW
   TESTAMENT, BROTHER
   OF JAMES

5) SPOKE, UTTERED SPEECH -
   RHYMES WITH "WALKED"

6) ANOTHER WORD FOR "I",
   JESUS SAID, "FOLLOW ___."

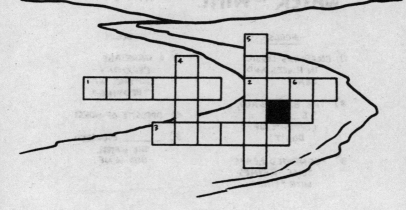

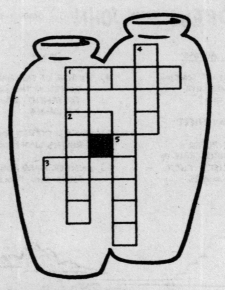

WATER to WINE

JOHN 2:1-11

ACROSS

1) COLORLESS LIQUID IN RIVERS AND SEAS

2) THE BRIDE SAID, "I ___." (OPPOSITE OF DON'T)

3) FERMENTED GRAPE JUICE - RHYMES WITH "FINE"

DOWN

1) A MARRIAGE CEREMONY - RHYMES WITH "BEDDING"

4) OPPOSITE OF WORST

5) _____ CHANGED THE WATER INTO WINE.

NICODEMUS

JOHN 3:1-21

ACROSS

1) TO COME INTO THIS
   WORLD - RHYMES
   WITH "HORN"

2) ANGRY

3) WE ARE BAPTIZED
   IN _____ (A
   CLEAR LIQUID).

4) FATHER, SON,
   HOLY _____

DOWN

1) A BASEBALL IS HIT
   WITH A _____.

5) MORE THAN ONCE -
   "YOU MUST BE
   BORN _____."

6) JESUS TOLD _____
   THAT HE MUST BE
   BORN AGAIN.

7) OPPOSITE OF DEATH

2) OPPOSITE OF WOMAN

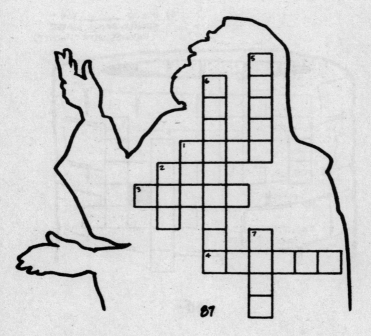

THE WOMAN AT THE WELL

JOHN 4:5-30

ACROSS

1) OPPOSITE OF MAN

2) ONE WHO SPEAKS FOR GOD

3) TO CONSUME A LIQUID - RHYMES WITH "THINK"

DOWN

1) A DEEP HOLE FROM WHICH WATER IS DRAWN - RHYMES WITH "FELL"

4) _____ COMES OUT OF A SPRING.

5) MANY TIMES, FREQUENTLY - RHYMES WITH "SOFTEN"

6) IF YOU _____, YOU SHOULD DRINK WATER (RHYMES WITH "FIRST").

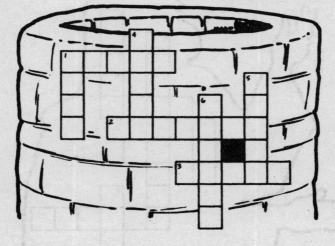

THE CITY of NAZARETH REJECTS JESUS

LUKE 4:16-30

ACROSS

1) JESUS GREW UP IN THE CITY OF _____.

2) JESUS LIVED THERE AS A ____ (OPPOSITE OF GIRL).

3) A LARGE TOWN - RHYMES WITH "PITY"

DOWN

4) THE LORD'S DAY, DAY OF REST

5) OPPOSITE OF IN

6) MAD, FULL OF ANGER

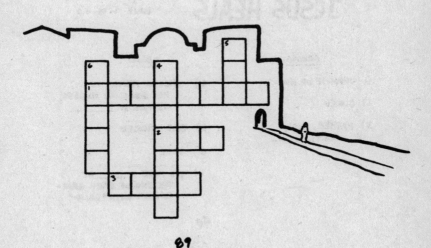

89

JESUS HEALS

LUKE 4:33-42

ACROSS

1) OPPOSITE OF HIM

2) CURED

3) FATHER, SON,
   HOLY _____

DOWN

4) WHEN A PERSON IS
   HOT FROM AN ILLNESS,
   HE HAS A _____.

5) BAD, WICKED

6) SICK

7) WE HAVE A ____ AT
   THE END OF EACH ARM-
   RHYMES WITH "SAND"

90

THE POOL OF BETHESDA

JOHN 5:1-16

ACROSS

1) OPPOSITE OF DOWN

2) OPPOSITE OF OUT OF

3) STROLLED, TRAVELED BY FOOT - RHYMES WITH "TALKED"

4) CURVED STRUCTURE ON A BUILDING - RHYMES WITH "PARCH"

DOWN

3) LABOR, EFFORT

5) POND, SMALL BODY OF WATER - RHYMES WITH "COOL"

6) ILLNESS, SICKNESS, AILMENT

JESUS CALLS MATTHEW MARK 2:13-14

ACROSS

1) WE USE THIS TO BUY THINGS

2) MONEY COLLECTED FROM THE PEOPLE BY THE GOVERNMENT - RHYMES WITH "FACTS"

3) HUMAN BEINGS, RACE, NATION - RHYMES WITH "STEEPLE"

DOWN

1) JESUS CALLED _____, THE TAX COLLECTOR, TO BE ONE OF HIS DESCIPLES.

4) ANOTHER WORD FOR "I" - JESUS SAID, "FOLLOW ___."

5) TO GO AFTER SOMEONE, "_____ THE LEADER" - RHYMES WITH "HOLLOW"

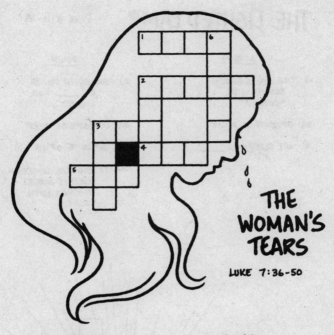

THE WOMAN'S TEARS

LUKE 7:36-50

ACROSS

1) THE WOMAN WASHED JESUS' _____ WITH HER TEARS.

2) OPPOSITE OF MAN (FEMALE)

3) OPPOSITE OF HERS

4) JESUS FORGAVE _____ SINS (OPPOSITE OF HIS).

5) TO BREAK GOD'S LAW

DOWN

2) TO CLEAN SOMETHING WITH WATER — _____ DISHES

3) LONG STRANDS THAT GROW ON OUR HEADS. RHYMES WITH "FAIR"

6) _____ COME FROM OUR EYES WHEN WE CRY.

THE LIGHTED LAMP

LUKE 8:16-18

ACROSS

1) THE WHOLE EARTH -
   RHYMES WITH
   "CURLED"

2) OPPOSITE OF DARK

3) WE SLEEP IN A _____.

DOWN

2) YOU BURN OIL IN
   A _____ FOR
   LIGHT

4) OPPOSITE OF OVER

5) OPPOSITE OF IN

6) TO CONCEAL SOMETHING,
   KEEP IT SECRET -
   RHYMES WITH
   "SIDE"

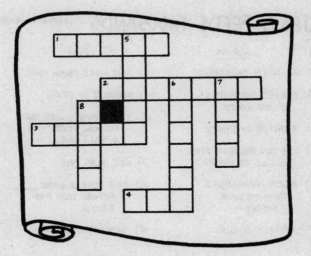

THE WOMAN
IN THE CROWD

MARK 5:22-34

ACROSS

1) TO MAKE PHYSICAL CONTACT - THE WOMAN REACHED TO _____ JESUS' ROBE (RHYMES WITH "MUCH").

2) PHYSICIANS

3) _____ RUNS THROUGH OUR VEINS

4) OPPOSITE OF HE

DOWN

5) A LARGE GROUP OF PEOPLE - RHYMES WITH "LOUD"

6) THE NUMBER AFTER ELEVEN

7) A LONG, FLOWING GARMENT - RHYMES WITH "LOBE"

8) OPPOSITE OF RICH

JESUS FEEDS THOUSANDS
MATTHEW 14:15-21

ACROSS

1) A WOVEN CONTAINER

2) FINNED CREATURES OF THE WATER

3) OPPOSITE OF EMPTY

4) THE BOY BROUGHT FIVE _____ OF BREAD.

5) PARTS, FRAGMENTS - RHYMES WITH "NIECES"

10) OPPOSITE OF GIRL

DOWN

2) ONE MORE THAN FOUR

4) OPPOSITE OF EARLY

6) JESUS FED _____ OF THE PEOPLE, EVERY SINGLE ONE.

7) ONE PLUS ONE

8) THE PEOPLE WERE _____ BEFORE THEY HAD EATEN.

9) OPPOSITE OF DOWN

96

PETER ON THE WATER

MATTHEW 14:28-31

ACROSS

1) JESUS SAID TO PETER, "_____."
   (RHYMES WITH "SOME")

2) OPPOSITE OF FLOAT

3) FULL OF FEAR

4) ANOTHER WORD FOR "I" –
   RHYMES WITH "BE"

DOWN

5) TO STROLL OR
   TRAVEL BY FOOT

6) _____ TRIED TO WALK
   ON WATER
   WITH JESUS.

7) MOVEMENT OF THE AIR –
   RHYMES WITH "SINNED"

8) TO RESCUE – RHYMES
   WITH "CAVE"

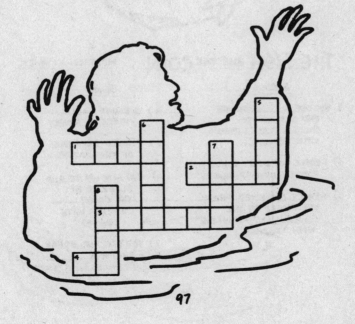

97

THE FISH AND THE COIN

MATTHEW 17:24-27

ACROSS

1) YOU USE A _____ ON THE END OF A LINE TO CATCH A FISH (RHYMES WITH "BOOK").

2) PEOPLE YOU DON'T KNOW— RHYMES WITH "RANGERS"

3) MONEY COLLECTED FROM THE PEOPLE BY THE GOVERNMENT — RHYMES WITH "SACKS"

DOWN

4) A ROUND, METAL PIECE OF MONEY

5) FINNED CREATURE OF THE WATER

6) YOU MIX WHITE AND BLACK TO GET THE COLOR _____ (RHYMES WITH "TRAY")

7) YOU EAT AND SPEAK WITH YOUR _____ (RHYMES WITH "SOUTH").

ADAM & EVE

GENESIS 2:15 - 3:24

ACROSS

1) THE _____ GUARDED THE GATE TO THE GARDEN.
2) IN SHAME, ADAM AND EVE _____ FROM GOD.
3) _____ WAS SECOND TO EAT THE FORBIDDEN FRUIT.
4) AFTER SINNING, ADAM AND EVE WERE SENT ____ OF THE GARDEN.
5) THE _____ TEMPTED EVE TO EAT THE FRUIT (SNAKE).

DOWN

1) ADAM NAMED THE _____.
3) EVE _____ THE FORBIDDEN FRUIT.
6) ADAM AND EVE WERE NOT TO EAT THE _____ OF THE TREE IN THE MIDDLE OF THE GARDEN.
7) THE SERPENT _____ TO EVE (DID NOT TELL THE TRUTH).

99

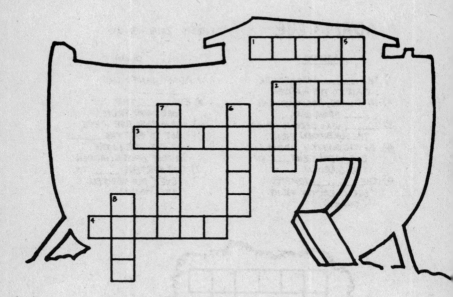

NOAH'S FAMILY BUILDS THE ARK

GENESIS 6:9-7:5

ACROSS

1) GOD SAID TO SEAL THE WOOD WITH _____.

2) NOAH'S SON

3) NOAH'S NEIGHBORS _____ AT NOAH AND HIS ARK.

4) GOD SAID TO USE THIS KIND OF WOOD TO BUILD THE ARK.

DOWN

2) NOT FRONT OR BACK, BUT _____

5) NOAH'S SON

6) THE ARK WAS _____ STORIES TALL INSIDE.

7) NOAH'S SON

8) GOD TOLD _____ HOW BIG TO BUILD THE ARK.

NOAH'S JOURNEY

GENESIS 7

ACROSS

1) WATER FALLING FROM THE SKY

2) GOD SAVED NOAH AND ALL HIS _____.

3) GOD SHUT THE _____ OF THE ARK.

4) THE DOVE CAME BACK TO NOAH WITH AN _____ BRANCH.

5) _____ COVERED ALL THE EARTH DURING THE FLOOD.

DOWN

1) GOD SET A _____ IN THE SKY AS A SIGN OF HIS PROMISE.

2) IT RAINED FOR _____ DAYS AND NIGHTS.

6) A BIRD NOAH SENT OUT FROM THE ARK - RHYMES WITH "LOVE"

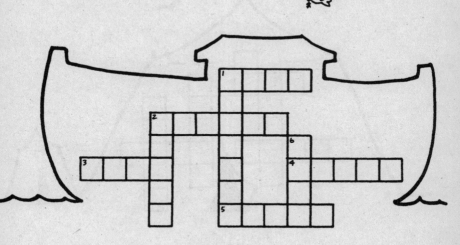

ABRAM'S JOURNEY

GENESIS 11:31 - 13:4

ACROSS

1) ABRAM'S WIFE

2) ABRAM'S FATHER

3) ABRAM AND HIS FAMILY JOURNEYED TO A FAR-AWAY _____.

DOWN

4) ABRAM LEFT THE CHALDEAN CITY OF _____.

5) SARAI'S HUSBAND.

6) FALSE GODS.

7) ABRAM'S FAMILY LIVED IN _____ FOR SHELTER AS THEY JOURNEYED.

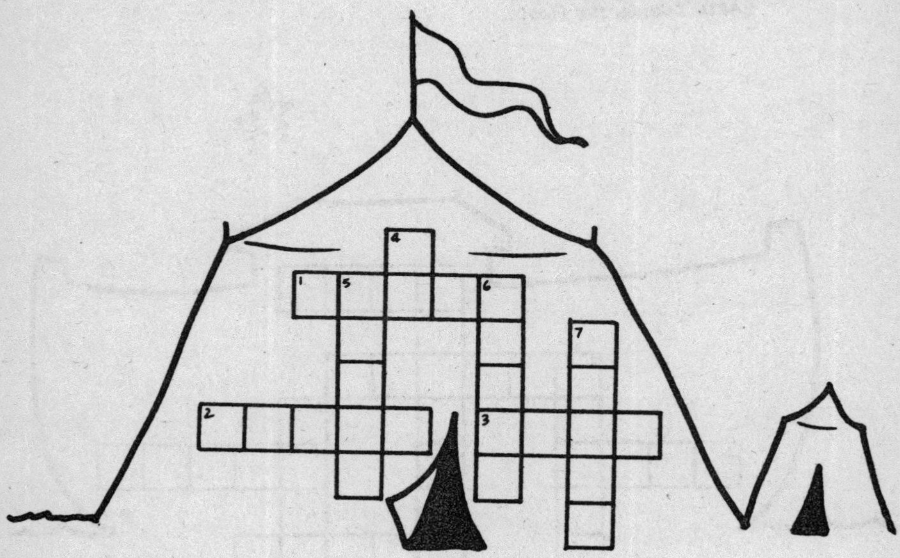

GOD'S COVENANT WITH ABRAHAM

GENESIS 15:1-18

ACROSS

1) GOD MADE A _____ TO GIVE ABRAM A SON.

2) ABRAM HAD NO _____.

DOWN

3) ABRAM LOVED ____ AND PROMISED TO SERVE HIM.

4) THE MANY LIGHTS IN THE NIGHT SKY.

5) ABRAM WAS NOW AN ____ MAN, NOT YOUNG.

6) GOD WOULD GIVE ABRAM AND SARAI A _____.

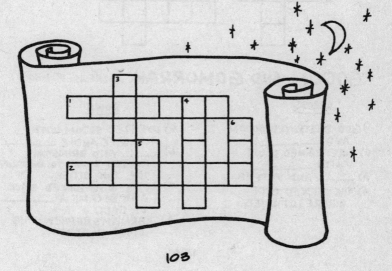

SODOM AND GOMORRAH GENESIS 19:1-30

ACROSS

1) GOD DESTROYED SODOM AND _____.
2) FIRE RAINED DOWN WITH _____.
3) _____ AND PEPPER.
4) THE WICKED CITY WHERE LOT LIVED.

DOWN

5) LOT FLED SODOM WITH HIS WIFE AND 2 _____.
6) _____ AND BRIMSTONE RAINED DOWN TO DESTROY THE TWO CITIES.
7) LOT'S WIFE LOOKED BACK AND BECAME A _____ OF SALT.
8) ABRAHAM'S NEPHEW WHO LIVED IN SODOM.

ISAAC'S BIRTH

GENESIS 21:1-8

ACROSS

1) THE SOUND OF LAUGHING.

2) ABRAHAM AND SARAH'S SON.

3) TALK TO GOD.

DOWN

4) ABRAHAM WAS 100 WHEN ISAAC WAS BORN. SARAH WAS ALSO VERY ____.

5) ISAAC GOT BIGGER. HE ____.

6) GOD ____ HIS PROMISES.

7) ISAAC'S MOTHER.

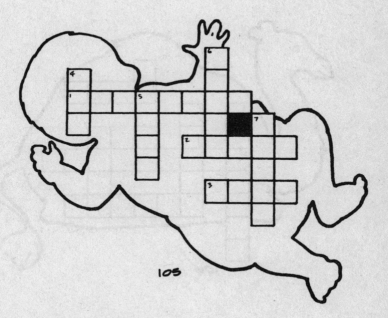

105

ISAAC'S BRIDE

ACROSS

1) ABRAHAM'S SERVANT GAVE REBEKAH A _____ TO WEAR ON HER FINGER...

2) ... AND 2 GOLD _____ TO WEAR ON HER WRISTS.

3) REBEKAH GAVE WATER TO THESE HUMP-BACKED ANIMALS.

DOWN

4) ISAAC'S WIFE.

5) ABRAHAM'S SON.

6) NEWLY MARRIED WOMAN. "HERE COMES THE _____."

7) REBEKAH DREW WATER FROM THE _____.

106

JACOB'S DREAM

ACROSS

1) A VISION DURING SLEEP
2) ROCK
3) GOD'S HEAVENLY MESSENGERS
4) WHAT YOU REST YOUR HEAD ON AT NIGHT AS YOU SLEEP.
5) GOD TOLD JACOB HE WOULD GIVE HIM THE _____ HE WAS LYING ON.
6) KIDS

DOWN

2) WHAT WE DO WHEN WE ARE TIRED AT NIGHT
7) HIGH DWELLING PLACE OF GOD
8) USED TO STEP UP ON TO REACH HIGH PLACES
9) FIRST- _____, BAND _____, HELP.

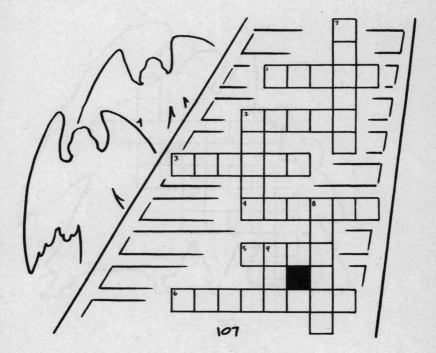

JACOB WRESTLES THE ANGEL

GENESIS 32:24-31

ACROSS

1) THE GRACE BEFORE A MEAL

2) TO STRETCH OUT FOR SOMETHING

3) A MESSENGER OF GOD.

DOWN

4) THE ANGEL TOUCHED JACOB'S _____.

5) JACOB'S NEW NAME

6) DAYBREAK, SUNRISE

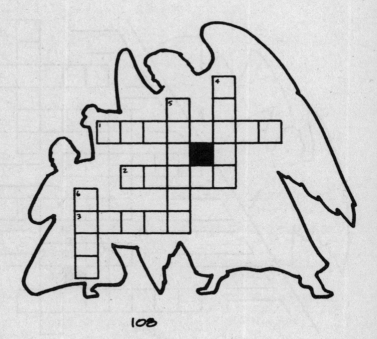

JOSEPH'S TROUBLE

GENESIS 37:15-35

ACROSS

1) JOSEPH'S OLDER BROTHER WHO TRIED TO PROTECT HIM

2) WHAT FLOWS THROUGH OUR VEINS

3) JOSEPH'S BROTHERS SOLD HIM AS A _____.

4) A LARGE, DEEP HOLE IN THE GROUND

5) JACOB WAS VERY _____ TO HEAR THAT HIS SON WAS DEAD.

DOWN

6) JOSEPH HAD ELEVEN _____.

7) TO LET SOMETHING FALL - RHYMES WITH "CROP"

8) JOSEPH AND HIS BROTHERS TENDED THEIR FATHER'S _____ OF SHEEP.

PHARAOH'S DREAM

GENESIS 41

ACROSS

1) A VISION DURING SLEEP

2) KING OF EGYPT

3) THE NUMBER AFTER "SIX"

4) IN WHAT MANNER?
   RHYMES WITH "COW"

5) OPPOSITE OF OUT

6) OVERWEIGHT

DOWN

5) NOT A HE, NOT A SHE, BUT AN ___

7) OPPOSITE OF POOR

8) OPPOSITE OF QUESTION

9) UNDERWEIGHT
   RHYMES WITH "PIN"

10) A CEREAL CROP, SUCH
    AS WHEAT. RHYMES
    WITH "TRAIN"

11) PLURAL OF FEMALE
    CATTLE

110

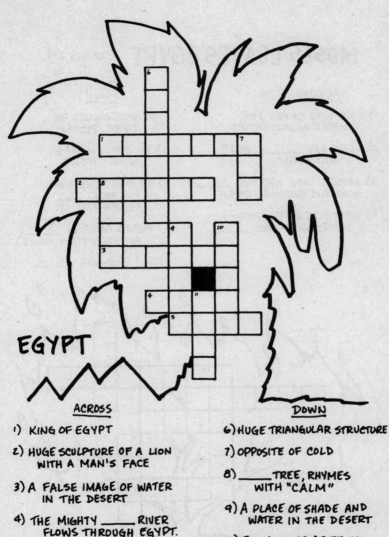

EGYPT

ACROSS

1) KING OF EGYPT

2) HUGE SCULPTURE OF A LION WITH A MAN'S FACE

3) A FALSE IMAGE OF WATER IN THE DESERT

4) THE MIGHTY _____ RIVER FLOWS THROUGH EGYPT.

5) THE DESERT HAS _____ DUNES

DOWN

6) HUGE TRIANGULAR STRUCTURE

7) OPPOSITE OF COLD

8) _____ TREE, RHYMES WITH "CALM"

9) A PLACE OF SHADE AND WATER IN THE DESERT

10) THE NUMBER AFTER SIX

11) A BABY SHEEP

111

MOSES LEAVES EGYPT

EXODUS 2:11

ACROSS

1) ONE WHO CARES FOR SHEEP AS MOSES DID

2) "LET MY _____ GO!", SAID GOD.

3) MOSES TOOK OFF HIS _____ AT THE BURNING BUSH.

8) OPPOSITE OF TOWARD — MOSES WENT FAR _____.

DOWN

1) PEOPLE OWNED BY OTHER PEOPLE

4) TO CUT, RHYMES WITH "NEW"

5) TO BUY SOMETHING YOU MUST ____ MONEY FOR IT.

6) MOSES ANGRILY _____ AN EGYPTIAN (KILLED).

7) THE BURNING _____

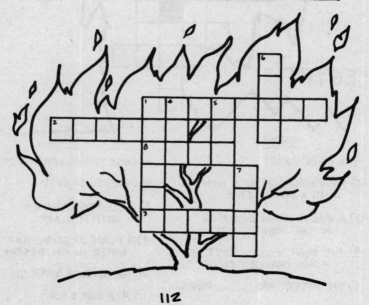

PASSOVER

EXODUS 12:1-36

<u>ACROSS</u>

1) A BABY SHEEP
2) THE ISRAELITES LEFT EGYPT QUICKLY, IN _____.
3) THEY ATE _____ HERBS WITH THEIR PASSOVER MEAL.
4) ONE TIME
5) THE ISRAELITES PUT _____ ON THEIR DOORPOSTS AS A SIGN FOR DEATH TO PASS BY THAT HOUSE.

<u>DOWN</u>

6) GOD SPARED THE FIRST-BORN OF THE HEBREWS ON THE NIGHT OF _____.
7) THE ISRAELITES ATE UNLEAVENED _____.
8) YOU MUST _____ RAW MEAT. RHYMES WITH "BOOK"

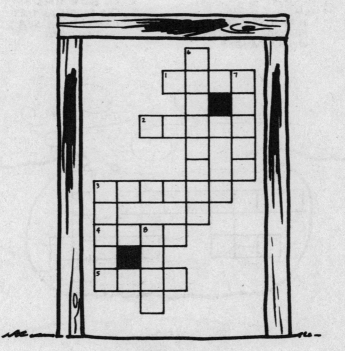

THE RED SEA

EXODUS 14

ACROSS

1) TWO-WHEELED WAR WAGONS DRAWN BY SWIFT HORSES

2) THE PEOPLE CROSSED THE RED SEA ON _____ LAND.

3) GOD _____ THE ISRAELITES FROM PHARAOH. RHYMES WITH "PAVED"

DOWN

4) PHARAOH'S GREAT_____ OF MEN AND CHARIOTS WAS DESTROYED.

5) THE RED _____

6) WALLS OF _____ WERE ON BOTH SIDES OF THE PEOPLE AS THEY CROSSED THE SEA ON DRY LAND.

WATER FROM THE ROCK

EXODUS 17:1-7

ACROSS

1) GOD TOLD MOSES TO
   _____ THE ROCK.
   RHYMES WITH "PIT"

2) THE MAN GOD CHOSE TO
   LEAD HIS PEOPLE
   FROM EGYPT

3) IF YOU ARE THIRSTY,
   HAVE SOMETHING
   TO _____.

4) OPPOSITE OF IN

DOWN

5) GOD'S PEOPLE WERE _____
   WITHOUT WATER
   TO DRINK

6) WATER CAME OUT OF
   THE _____ AFTER
   MOSES HIT IT.

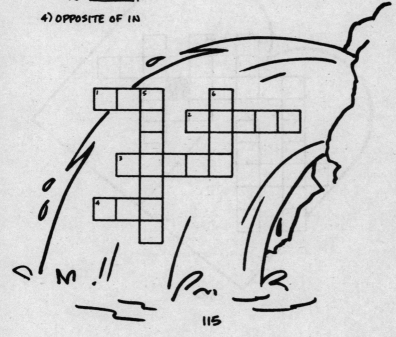

115

THE TEN COMMANDMENTS EXODUS 20:1-17

ACROSS

1) FALSE GODS

2) TO TAKE FROM SOMEONE
   WITHOUT PERMISSION

3) OPPOSITE OF TRUTH

4) DO NOT USE GOD'S
   NAME IN _____.
   (RHYMES WITH "RAIN")

DOWN

2) KEEP THE _____ DAY

5) THERE IS ONLY ____ GOD.

6) "THOU SHALL NOT ____."

7) "THOU SHALL NOT _____
   THY NEIGHBOR'S GOODS."

8) "_____ THY MOTHER AND
   FATHER."

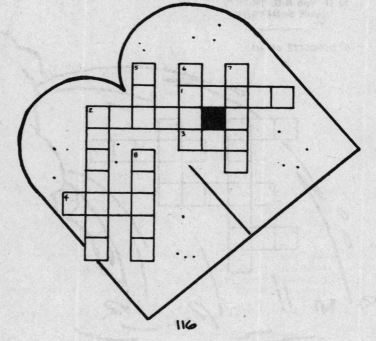

116

THE TABERNACLE

EXODUS 25,26

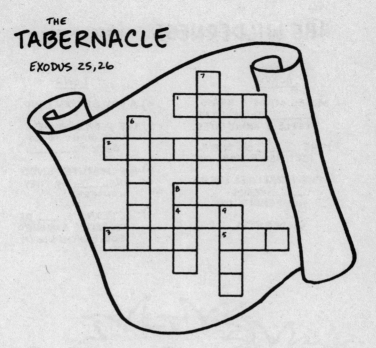

ACROSS

1) THE COLOR OF THE SKY

2) LARGE PIECES OF CLOTH HUNG AROUND THE TABERNACLE

3) A BRIDE WEARS THIS OVER HER FACE, THE CURTAIN BEFORE THE HOLY OF HOLIES.

4) THE LAMPS BURNED _____.

5) _____ OF THE COVENANT

DOWN

6) COLOR OF GRAPE SODA COLOR OF ROYALTY

7) SACRIFICES WERE BURNED ON AN _____.

8) PRECIOUS YELLOW METAL

9) BURNS OIL FOR LIGHT

THE WILDERNESS

NUMBERS 14:20-24

ACROSS

1) MOSES MADE A BRASS _____ TO HEAL THE PEOPLE'S SNAKE BITES.

2) THE _____ ON THEIR FEET NEVER WORE OUT.

3) THE ISRAELITES SPENT _____ YEARS WANDERING IN THE WILDERNESS.

DOWN

4) A DRY BARREN LAND

5) THE PEOPLE WHINED, " WE WANT TO GO BACK TO _____ . "

6) THE ISRAELITES LIVED IN _____ AS THEY WANDERED.

7) THE PEOPLE'S ____ OF UNBELIEF ANGERED GOD. (RHYMES WITH "FIN")

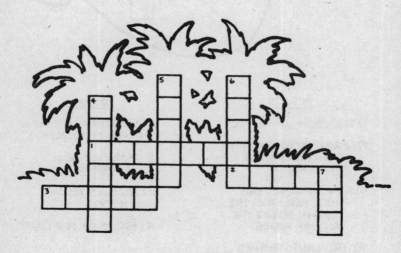

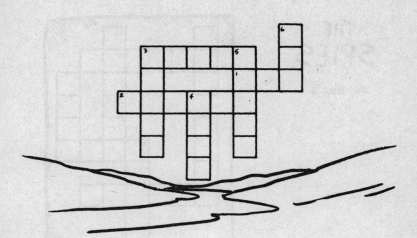

THE PROMISED LAND
DEUTERONOMY 34

ACROSS

1) MOSES WAS 120 YEARS ____ WHEN HE DIED.

2) THE PEOPLE HAD TO CROSS THE ____ RIVER TO ENTER CANAAN. (STARTS WITH J, ENDS WITH N)

3) A BASEBALL MIT IS MADE TO ____ THE BALL.

DOWN

3) MOSES WAS NOT ALLOWED TO ____ THE RIVER JORDAN.

4) MOSES ____ BEFORE THE PEOPLE ENTERED THE PROMISED LAND (PASSED AWAY).

5) THE LAND WAS FLOWING WITH MILK AND ____.

6) ____ BURIED MOSES BECAUSE THE PEOPLE HAD ALL LEFT FOR THE PROMISED LAND.

THE SPIES

JOSHUA 2

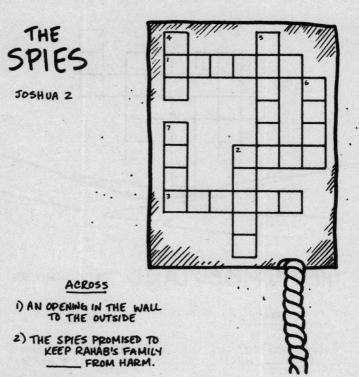

ACROSS

1) AN OPENING IN THE WALL TO THE OUTSIDE

2) THE SPIES PROMISED TO KEEP RAHAB'S FAMILY _____ FROM HARM.

3) RELATIVES

DOWN

2) SECRET AGENTS (RHYMES WITH "FLIES")

4) THE NUMBER THAT COMES AFTER "ONE"

5) GOD PUT _____ IN CHARGE OF THE PEOPLE AFTER MOSES DIED.

6) RAHAB PUT A LONG, RED _____ OUT HER WINDOW FOR THE SPIES TO CLIMB DOWN TO SAFETY.

7) THE TOP OF A HOUSE

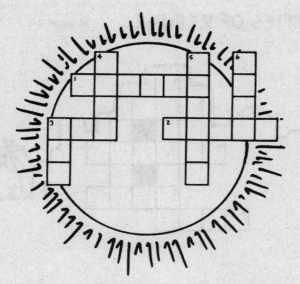

GOD FIGHTS FOR JOSHUA AND HIS PEOPLE
JOSHUA 10:8-14

ACROSS

1) THE MAN WHO LED ISRAEL AFTER MOSES DIED

2) THE SUN STOOD _____, NOT MOVING.

3) THE "LIGHT HOLDER" OF DAYTIME (RHYMES WITH "RUN")

DOWN

3) THE SPACE HIGH OVER HEAD - RHYMES WITH "PIE"

4) "LIGHT HOLDER" OF THE NIGHT (RHYMES WITH "SOON")

5) A FIGHT BETWEEN ARMIES

6) CHUNKS OF ICE FALLING FROM THE SKY LIKE RAIN

CITIES OF REFUGE

JOSHUA 20

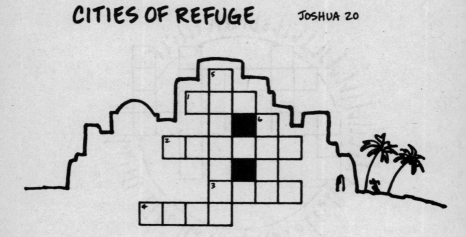

ACROSS

1) OPPOSITE OF LIVE
   RHYMES WITH "TIE"

2) LARGE TOWNS

3) TO TAKE A LIFE

4) PROTECTED FROM
   HARM

DOWN

5) AN ERROR

6) "ALIVE AND _____"
   RHYMES WITH
   "SELL"

JUDGES

JUDGES 3

ACROSS

1) OPPOSITE OF UP

2) GOD WOULD SEND JUDGES TO _____ HIS PEOPLE FROM THEIR ENEMIES.

3) THE PEOPLE WORSHIPED IDOLS, OR _____ GODS.

4) THE PEOPLE _____ THEIR PROMISE TO SERVE GOD AND SINNED.

DOWN

5) PLURAL OF JUDGE

6) THE PEOPLE WOULD _____ DOWN BEFORE IDOLS.

7) OPPOSITE OF YES

8) THE PEOPLE DID _____ IN THE SIGHT OF THE LORD. (WICKEDNESS)

9) OPPOSITE OF STRONG

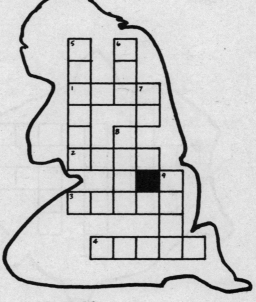

123

GIDEON

JUDGES 6

ACROSS

1) ANIMALS THAT GRAZE
   EAT GREEN _____.

2) AN ANGEL SPOKE TO
   GIDEON FROM UNDER
   A _____ OAK TREE.
   (OPPOSITE OF SMALL)

3) OPPOSITE OF WET

4) SHEEPSKIN, WOOL —
   RHYMES WITH
   "PEACE"

DOWN

1) GOD CHOSE _____ TO
   SAVE HIS PEOPLE
   FROM THE
   MIDIANITES.

3) WATER DROPLETS ON
   GRASS IN THE
   MORNING

5) MESSENGER OF GOD

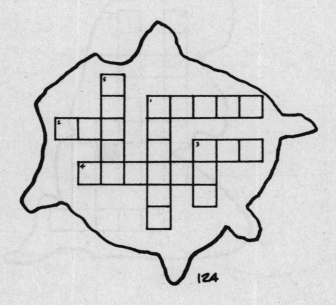

124

YOUNG SAMSON

JUDGES 13

ACROSS

1) BOY CHILD - RHYMES
   WITH "FUN"

2) KIDS

3) HIS LONG HAIR GAVE
   HIM HIS STRENGTH

DOWN

4) GOD'S MESSENGER

5) TO CUT A LITTLE -
   RHYMES WITH "BRIM"

6) TO SWALLOW A LIQUID

7) SAMSON'S _____
   GREW LONG.

RUTH

ACROSS

1) BOAZ MARRIED RUTH AND SHE BECAME HIS _____.

2) RUTH _____ HER MOTHER-IN-LAW, NAOMI, WITH HER WHOLE HEART.

3) _____ FELL IN LOVE WITH RUTH AND MARRIED HER.

4) OPPOSITE OF OUT

DOWN

1) AN OWL ASKS, "_____?".

2) RUTH PROMISED TO NEVER _____ NAOMI.

4) RUTH'S MOTHER-IN-LAW

5) BOAZ LET RUTH GATHER GRAIN IN HIS MANY _____.

6) OPPOSITE OF BEGIN

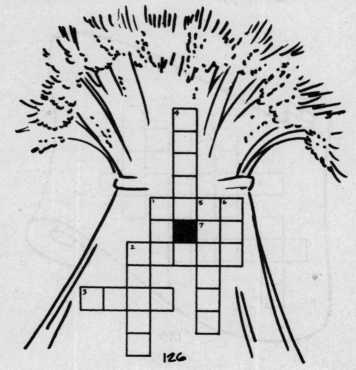

126

YOUNG SAMUEL
AND ELI

1 SAMUEL 1:24 – 2:21

ACROSS

1) SAMUEL HAD 3 BROTHERS AND 2 _____.

2) 365 DAYS

7) WHAT A CAT SAYS

DOWN

3) THE PRIEST WHO TOOK CARE OF SAMUEL

4) A JACKET

5) SAMUEL GOT BIGGER, HE _____.

6) HANNAH'S FIRST SON

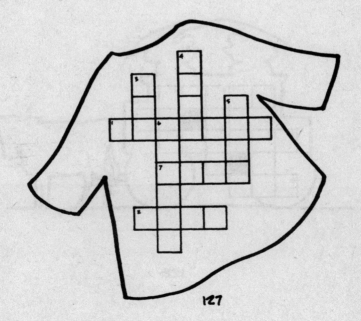

127

THE ARK STOLEN! I SAMUEL 4-6

ACROSS

1) A LARGE CART PULLED BY ANIMALS

2) LARGE, STRONG CATTLE

3) TO BE FULL OF FEAR

4) _____ OF THE COVENANT

DOWN

5) HAPPY - RHYMES WITH "PLAID"

6) TO MOVE THE HEAD UP AND DOWN, RHYMES WITH "GOD"

7) NOT CLOSE - RHYMES WITH "CAR"

128

SAUL, A KING
FOR ISRAEL

1 SAMUEL 8-10

ACROSS

1) SAM IS SHORT FOR THE NAME _____.

2) YOU MAKE A SANDWICH WITH TWO SLICES OF _____.

3) A MALE RULER OF A COUNTRY. SAUL WAS ISRAEL'S FIRST _____.

DOWN

1) THE MEN _____ A SONG WITH THEIR VOICES.

4) OPPOSITE OF UNDER

5) SAMUEL POURED OIL ON TOP OF SAUL'S _____ TO ANOINT HIM.

6) ISRAEL'S FIRST KING

7) THEY BURNED _____ IN THEIR LAMPS.

YOUNG DAVID 1 SAMUEL 16

ACROSS

1) DAVID PLAYED _____ ON HIS HARP. (RHYMES WITH "THONGS")

2) DAVID HAD HOW MANY BROTHERS? (THE NUMBER AFTER SIX)

3) OPPOSITE OF STOP

4) THE STRINGED INSTRUMENT THAT DAVID PLAYED

5) SAMUEL POURED _____ ON DAVID'S HEAD TO ANOINT HIM.

DOWN

6) OPPOSITE OF OLD

7) DAVID WAS A SHEPHERD OVER HIS FATHER'S FLOCK OF _____.

8) DAVID WOULD PLAY SOOTHING MUSIC FOR KING _____.

9) GOD CHOSE _____ TO BE KING AFTER SAUL.

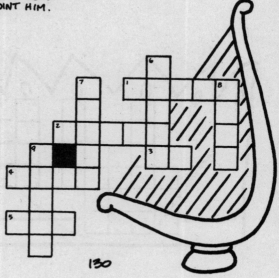

130

DAVID AND JONATHAN 1 SAMUEL 18:1-4

ACROSS

1) _____ AND ARROW

2) SAUL'S SON

3) JONATHAN AND DAVID WERE BEST _____.

4) JONATHAN'S FATHER

DOWN

1) DAVID AND JONATHAN LOVED EACH OTHER AS IF THEY WERE _____.

5) MEN SHAKE _____ WHEN THEY FIRST MEET. (RHYMES WITH "SANDS")

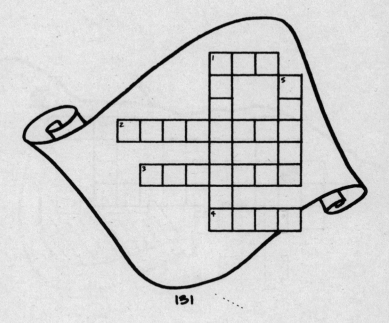

131

DAVID FLEES SAUL
1 SAMUEL 19

ACROSS

1) KING _____ WAS ANGRY WITH DAVID

2) OPPOSITE OF SWEET

3) OPPOSITE OF LOVED

4) SAUL BECAME AN _____ OF DAVID'S, A FOE.

DOWN

5) "_____ AND SEEK"

6) DAVID TRIED TO GET FAR _____ FROM ANGRY SAUL.

7) DAVID _____ AWAY FROM KING SAUL

8) OPPOSITE OF HAPPY

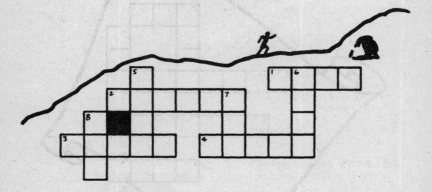

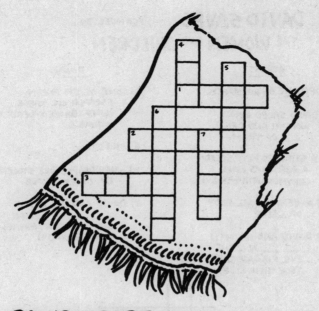

DAVID SPARES SAUL I SAMUEL 24

ACROSS

1) STOLE (RHYMES WITH "BOOK")

2) A PART (RHYMES WITH "NIECE")

3) DAVID DID NOT WANT TO HURT KING _____.

DOWN

4) DAVID _____ OFF A PIECE OF KING SAUL'S ROYAL ROBE WITH A KNIFE.

5) KING SAUL WORE A _____ (LIKE "BATH _____").

6) DAVID COULD HAVE _____ KING SAUL, BUT HE DIDN'T.

7) KING SAUL WENT INTO A _____ IN A MOUNTAIN. (RHYMES WITH "SAVE")

DAVID SAVES
THE WOMEN AND CHILDREN

1 SAMUEL 30

ACROSS

1) OPPOSITE OF HUSBANDS

2) DAVID SAVED EVERY
WOMAN AND CHILD,
_____ OF THEM.

3) A STICK TO HELP STEADY
A PERSON'S WALK
(RHYMES WITH "LANE")

4) A VERY SMALL BODY
OF WATER

5) DAVID AND HIS MEN
_____ ALL THE
EVIL KIDNAPPERS,
TOOK THEIR LIVES.

DOWN

3) SOME OF THE ENEMY
ESCAPED ON THESE
HUMP-BACKED DESERT
ANIMALS.

5) CHILDREN

6) WHEN PEOPLE ARE STOLEN
BY OTHER PEOPLE

7) DAVID AND HIS ARMY
_____ THE WOMEN
AND CHILDREN (RHYMES
WITH "PAVED").

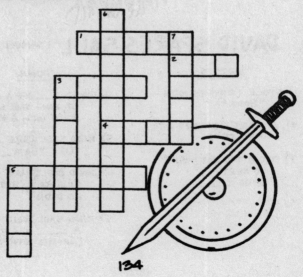

134

KING DAVID

2 SAMUEL 5:1-5

ACROSS

1) DAVID BECAME KING AFTER KING _____ DIED.

2) DAVID CRIED WHEN HE HEARD OF THE DEATH OF HIS BEST _____, JONATHAN.

3) HOW MANY TRIBES IN THE NATION OF ISRAEL?

4) NOW ISRAEL WOULD BE RULED BY _____, THE NEW KING.

DOWN

1) OPPOSITE OF HAPPY

5) A KING WEARS THIS ON HIS HEAD.

6) OPPOSITE OF BEGIN

7) A MAN WHO RULES OVER A COUNTRY (RHYMES WITH "RING")

8) A DEEP HOLE IN THE GROUND WHERE WATER CAN BE DRAWN.

DAVID BRINGS PEACE 2 SAMUEL 8,9

ACROSS

1) OPPOSITE OF SAD

2) LONG BATTLES BETWEEN NATIONS

3) A BUILDING THAT PEOPLE LIVE IN (RHYMES WITH "MOUSE")

4) OPPOSITE OF DOWN

DOWN

5) NO WARS OR FIGHTING

6) DAVID WAS VICTORIOUS AND ____ THE WARS HE FOUGHT.

7) DAVID TOOK CARE OF JONATHAN'S SON, AS HE PROMISED KING ____ THAT HE WOULD (RHYMES WITH "PAUL").

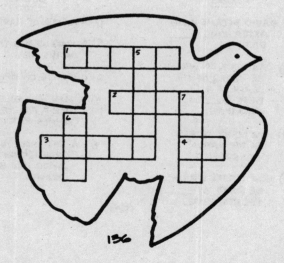

136

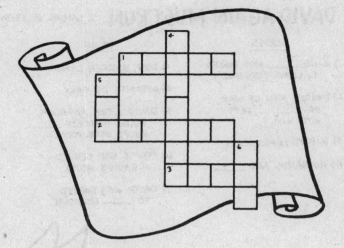

NATHAN AND DAVID   2 SAMUEL 12:1-14

ACROSS

1) REMORSEFUL, TO FEEL
   REGRET - RHYMES
   WITH "GLORY"

2) THE PROPHET WHO
   SHOWED DAVID
   HIS SIN

3) IT WAS WRONG FOR
   KING DAVID TO _____
   ANOTHER MAN'S WIFE.
   (RHYMES WITH "LAKE")

DOWN

4) ONE WHO SPEAKS FOR
   GOD. NATHAN WAS
   A _____.

5) TO DISOBEY GOD -
   RHYMES WITH "FIN"

6) NATHAN MADE DAVID
   _____ (LOOK AT) HIS
   OWN GREAT SIN.

157

DAVID AGAIN MUST RUN 2 SAMUEL 15:13-30

ACROSS

1) KING _____ WAS FORCED TO LEAVE JERUSALEM.

2) DAVID'S MEN OF WAR, OR _____, LEFT WITH HIM.

3) RIPPED, SHREDDED

4) HUSBANDS AND _____

DOWN

1) DRY, BARREN LAND

2) OPPOSITE OF FAST

5) DAVID'S SON, ABSALOM, MADE HIMSELF _____, RULER OVER ISRAEL.

6) PEOPLE WHO SERVED IN DAVID'S HOUSE.

7) DAVID WAS FORCED TO _____ HIS HOME.

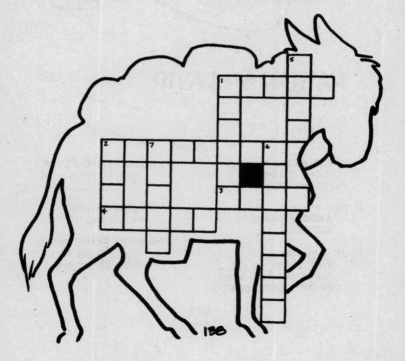

138

DAVID'S SON, ABSALOM, DIES

2 SAMUEL 18

ACROSS

1) A STAND OF MANY TREES

2) DAVID'S ARMY WAS VICTORIOUS. THEY _____ THE BATTLE.

3) WEPT

4) ABSALOM'S HAIR WAS VERY _____, NOT SHORT.

DOWN

5) DAVID COULD SEE THE MESSENGERS _____ QUICKLY TOWARDS HIM.

6) ABSALOM GOT HIS HAIR CAUGHT IN THE BRANCHES OF A _____.

139

DAVID'S LAST YEARS

ACROSS

1) WE _____ ON CHAIRS

2) NUMERAL, SUCH AS _____ ONE. (RHYMES WITH "LUMBER")

3) ROCK

4) KING DAVID WORSHIPED _____ AND LOVED HIM.

DOWN

5) SACRIFICES WOULD BE OFFERED ON AN _____.

6) DAVID ORDERED HIS HELPERS TO _____ HOW MANY MEN WERE IN ISRAEL.

7) OPPOSITE OF YOUNG

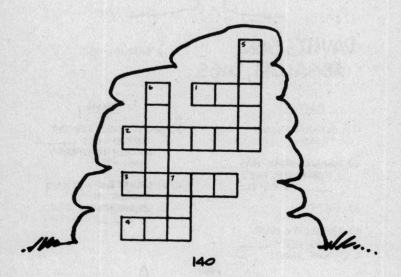

140

KING SOLOMON

I KINGS 2:1-11

ACROSS

1) THE NATION SOLOMON RULED OVER

2) A KING _____ ON HIS THRONE (RHYMES WITH "FITS").

3) SOLOMON WAS A _____ MAN, NOT OLD.

DOWN

4) DAVID _____ SOON AFTER SOLOMON WAS MADE KING. (OPPOSITE OF LIVED)

5) THE NUMBER AFTER NINETEEN

6) OPPOSITE OF WOMAN

7) SOLOMON WAS DAVID AND BATHSHEBA'S _____.

ONE BABY
TWO MOTHERS

1 KINGS 3:16-28

ACROSS

1) TO DIVIDE SOMETHING USING A SHARP BLADE - RHYMES WITH "HUT"

2) TO BE VERY WISE IS TO HAVE _____.

3) TO CUT INTO PIECES - RHYMES WITH "ASIDE"

4) OPPOSITE OF FROM

DOWN

1) OFFSPRING - RHYMES WITH "WILD"

5) THE NUMBER AFTER THE NUMBER ONE

6) WHEN SOMETHING IS BOUGHT, IT IS _____ (RHYMES WITH "GOLD").

7) OPPOSITE OF FATHER

8) OPPOSITE OF OUT

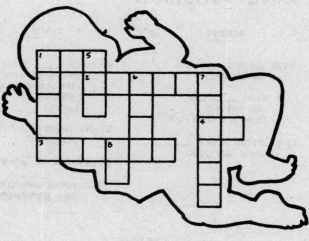

142

QUEEN OF SHEBA

I KINGS 10:1-13

ACROSS

1) QUEEN OF _____

2) A HUMP-BACKED DESERT ANIMAL

3) OPPOSITE OF OLD

4) PRECIOUS YELLOW METAL

5) WEALTHY

DOWN

1) _____ WAS FULL OF WISDOM.

6) THE _____ OF SHEBA VISITED SOLOMON.

7) THE QUEEN OF SHEBA CAME FROM A _____ AWAY LAND

8) RICHES

143

THE KINGDOM DIVIDES
ISRAEL & JUDAH

1 KINGS 12:16-33

ACROSS

1) THE NUMBER THAT
   FOLLOWS AFTER NINE

2) A MAN WHO RULES
   A COUNTRY

3) COUNSEL GIVEN TO
   HELP SOMEONE
   MAKE A DECISION
   (ENDS WITH -ICE)

4) ONE OF TWO PARTS
   (RHYMES WITH
   "CALF")

DOWN

1) ISRAEL DIVIDED ITS
   TWELVE _____
   INTO TWO
   KINGDOMS.

5) THE KINGDOM WAS
   DIVIDED INTO
   ISRAEL AND _____.

6) THE NEW KINGS DID
   NOT SEEK _____.

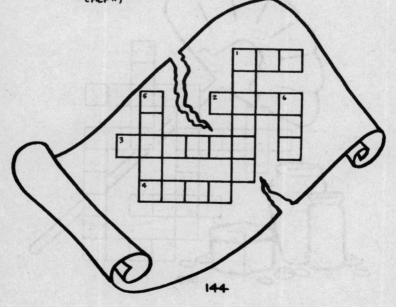

ELIJAH RAISES THE WIDOW'S SON

1 KINGS 17:8-24

ACROSS

1) OPPOSITE OF LAST

2) A WOMAN WHOSE HUSBAND HAS DIED

3) TO TALK TO GOD

DOWN

1) GRAIN GROUND TO A POWDER - RHYMES WITH "HOUR"

4) LAMPS BURN _____ FOR LIGHT.

5) ILL, AILING

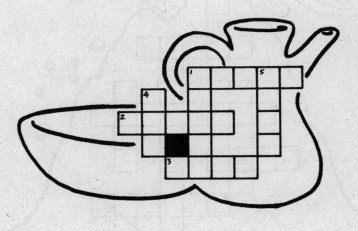

ELIJAH FLEES JEZEBEL

1 KINGS 19:1-18

ACROSS

1) A MESSENGER OF GOD

2) TALL PEAK ON THE LAND

3) STONE

4) FIRE - RHYMES WITH "GAMES"

DOWN

5) TO SWALLOW A LIQUID

6) WHEN THE GROUND SHAKES

7) YOU SPEAK WITH YOUR _____ (RHYMES WITH "CHOICE").

8) THE MOVEMENT OF AIR - RHYMES WITH "PINNED"

9) TO CONSUME FOOD

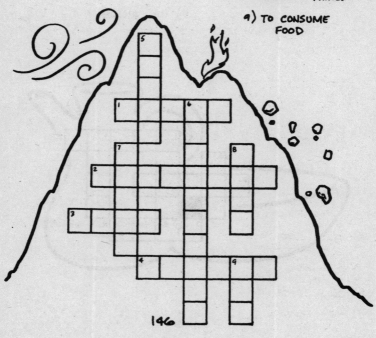

146

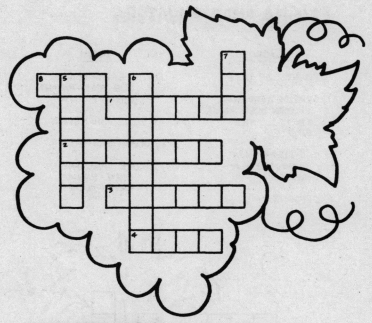

EVIL JEZEBEL   1 KINGS 21

ACROSS

1) JEZEBEL _____ THE
   VINEYARD'S OWNER
   (TOOK HIS LIFE).

2) _____ WAS A
   WICKED WOMAN.

3) RELATIVES

4) _____ CHASE CATS.

8) YOU SLEEP IN A _____.

DOWN

5) THE PROPHET WHO
   THE RAVENS FED

6) A FARM WHERE GRAPES
   ARE GROWN

7) OPPOSITE OF GOOD

147

ELISHA AND THE WATERS 2 KINGS 3

ACROSS

1) OPPOSITE OF TAKE

2) ISRAEL'S ARMY HAD VICTORY OVER MOAB. THEY _____ THE BATTLE.

3) THE LIQUID THAT FLOWS FROM A SPRING

4) OPPOSITE OF LIFE

DOWN

1) THE EARTH UNDER OUR FEET - RHYMES WITH "POUND"

5) _____ AND PEPPER

6) OPPOSITE OF BITTER

7) MORE THAN ONE MAN - RHYMES WITH "TEN"

148

A BOY IS HEALED

2 KINGS
4:8-37

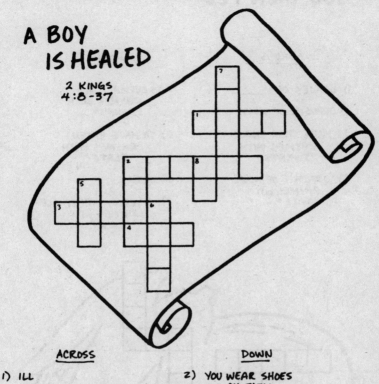

ACROSS

1) ILL

2) OPPOSITE OF MOTHER

3) THE MOTHER _____ HER BOY WITH ALL HER HEART.

4) TO BIND SOMETHING WITH STRING OR ROPE - RHYMES WITH "LIE"

DOWN

2) YOU WEAR SHOES ON THEM

5) OPPOSITE OF GIRL

6) OPPOSITE OF LIVED

7) THE BOY WAS _____ AGAIN! (OPPOSITE OF DEAD)

8) OPPOSITE OF SHE

149

100 MEN FED

2 KINGS 4:42-44

ACROSS

1) LOAVES OF _____

2) OPPOSITE OF WOMEN

3) MORE THAN ENOUGH -
   RHYMES WITH
   "TWENTY"

4) OPPOSITE OF NONE -
   RHYMES WITH
   "TALL"

DOWN

2) SEVERAL, ALOT -
   RHYMES WITH
   "PENNY"

5) TO HAVE EATEN
   RHYMES WITH
   "PLATE"

6) SPEAK

7) A YELLOW VEGETABLE -
   RHYMES WITH
   "HORN"

150

THE LOST AXHEAD 2 KINGS 6:1-7

ACROSS

1) THE AXHEAD DROPPED AND _____ INTO THE WATER (RHYMES WITH "WELL").

2) SOMETHING WOODEN IS MADE OF _____.

3) OPPOSITE OF "OUT OF"

4) CLEAR LIQUID FLOWING IN A RIVER

DOWN

1) OPPOSITE OF SINK - RHYMES WITH "BOAT"

5) OPPOSITE OF IN

6) TOOL USED FOR CHOPPING WOOD - RHYMES WITH "TAX"

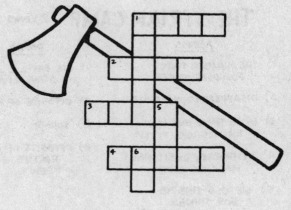

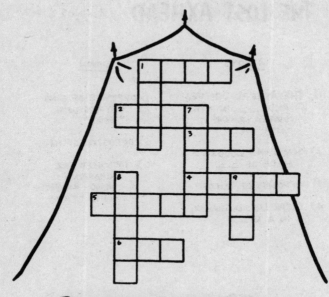

THE SYRIAN CAMP 2 KINGS 7

ACROSS

1) THE NUMBER THAT FOLLOWS THREE

2) DISAPPEARED, VANISHED

3) MORE THAN ONE MAN - RHYMES WITH "TEN"

4) TEMPORARY DWELLINGS MADE OF CLOTH

5) WE USE THIS TO BUY THINGS.

6) TO LOOK - RHYMES WITH "TEA"

DOWN

1) WE EAT _____ TO STAY ALIVE.

7) OPPOSITE OF FULL

8) SOUND

9) OPPOSITE OF OLD - RHYMES WITH "FEW"

THE SAMARITANS
AND THE LIONS

2 KINGS 17:24-41

ACROSS

1) LARGE, MANED CATS

2) NATIONS

3) ROADS THROUGH TOWN - RHYMES WITH "TREATS"

4) LARGE TOWN

DOWN

5) FALSE GODS

6) ONLY A _____ COULD OFFER SACRIFICES OR ENTER THE TABERNACLE. (RHYMES WITH "FEAST")

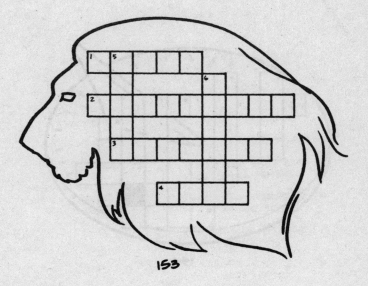

153

HEZEKIAH SPARED

ACROSS

1) OPPOSITE OF DIE

2) A DEVICE WHICH TELLS TIME USING THE SHADOW CAST BY THE SUN

3) OPPOSITE OF UP

4) TO QUESTION— RHYMES WITH "TASK"

DOWN

5) ILL

6) WHEN WE CRY _____ FALL FROM OUR EYES.

7) THE BRIGHT SUN CASTS THE TREE'S _____ ON THE LAWN. (SHADE CAST BY AN OBJECT)

8) TALK TO GOD

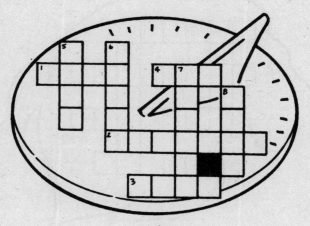

154

KING MANASSEH   2 KINGS 21:1-26

ACROSS

1) FALSE GODS

2) BROKE GOD'S LAW - RHYMES WITH "PINNED"

3) "LIGHT HOLDER" OF THE NIGHT SKY - RHYMES WITH "SOON"

DOWN

2) "LIGHT HOLDER" OF THE DAY - RHYMES WITH "FUN"

4) OPPOSITE OF GOOD

5) MANASSEH _____ MANY INNOCENT PEOPLE (TOOK THEIR LIVES).

6) OPPOSITE OF YES

JEHOSHAPHAT, A GOOD KING

2 CHRONICLES 20:1-21

ACROSS

1) _____ WAS A GOOD KING.

2) A MAN WHO RULES A COUNTRY

3) YOU USE A ____ TO UNLOCK A LOCK.

DOWN

4) THE PEOPLE SANG ____ OF PRAISE TO THE LORD.

5) GRATITUDE

6) JEHOSHAPHAT WOULD ____ TO GOD OFTEN, TALK TO HIM.

7) JEHOSHAPHAT LOVED GOD WITH HIS WHOLE ____ .

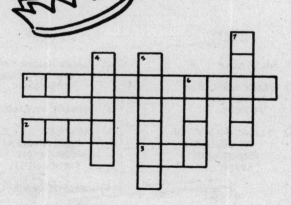

156

JOASH RESTORES THE TEMPLE

2 CHRONICLES 24:1-14

ACROSS

1) THE NUMBER AFTER THE NUMBER SIX

2) FIX

3) OPPOSITE OF OLD - RHYMES WITH "FEW"

4) LARGE RECTANGULAR CONTAINER - RHYMES WITH "FOX"

DOWN

5) HOUSE OF WORSHIP

6) THE BOX WAS MADE OF LUMBER, OR _____ (RHYMES WITH "GOOD").

7) OPPOSITE OF OUT

157

KING UZZIAH'S SIN   2 CHRONICLES 26:16-21

ACROSS

1) OPPOSITE OF OUT

2) OPPOSITE OF BEFORE

3) SERIOUS SKIN DISEASE

4) ONLY THE _____ COULD GO INTO THE HOLY PLACE TO BURN THE INCENSE.

DOWN

5) AN AROMATIC SUBSTANCE BURNED FOR FRAGRANCE

6) THE PART OF THE FACE BETWEEN THE EYEBROWS AND HAIRLINE

7) SET APART TO GOD— _____ OF HOLIES

158

REBUILDING THE TEMPLE

EZRA 3:8-13

ACROSS

1) A STRIP OF LEATHER OR CLOTH TIED AROUND THE WAIST.

2) WEPT

3) ROCKS - RHYMES WITH "PHONES"

4) OPPOSITE OF LAST

DOWN

1) ONES WHO BUILD THINGS

5) HAPPY, JOYFUL - RHYMES WITH "HAD"

6) WE ____ ON CHAIRS - RHYMES WITH HIT

159

THE TEMPLE FINISHED

EZRA 6:13-18

ACROSS

1) SET APART TO GOD —
   ____ OF HOLIES

2) TO COMPLETE, TO
   GET DONE

3) THE NUMBER
   BEFORE
   THREE

DOWN

4) OPPOSITE OF BEGIN

5) THOSE WHO SPEAK FOR
   GOD — HAGGAI AND
   ZECHARIAH WERE ____.

6) HAPPINESS, GREAT GLADNESS

7) PRECIOUS YELLOW METAL

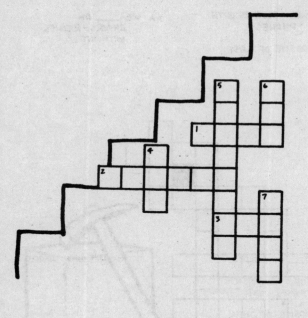

160

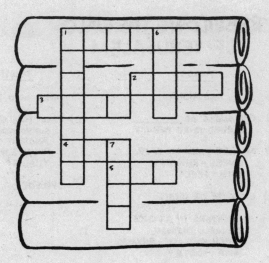

EZRA KEEPS GOD'S BOOK EZRA

ACROSS

1) ONE WHO COPIED BOOKS AND DID THE JOB OF WRITING THINGS DOWN - RHYMES WITH "BRIBE"

2) DUPLICATE, REPRODUCTION RHYMES WITH "POPPY"

3) SET APART TO GOD - ____ OF HOLIES

4) A RULE, A STATUTE RHYMES WITH "PAW"

5) OPPOSITE OF NEW

DOWN

1) ROLLS WHICH HAVE BEEN WRITTEN ON - RHYMES WITH "ROLLS"

6) MANY PAGES BOUND TOGETHER IS A ____ - RHYMES WITH "COOK"

7) "THE ____ OF GOD " - RHYMES WITH HEARD

161

REBUILDING THE WALLS OF JERUSALEM

NEHEMIAH 2-5

ACROSS

1) _____ AND ARROW

2) THE WALLS OF _____ NEEDED TO BE REBUILT

3) TO GET DOWN ON YOUR KNEES - RHYMES WITH "FEEL"

4) OPPOSITE OF NIGHT

5) AN OPENING IN A FENCE OR WALL THROUGH WHICH TO WALK - RHYMES WITH "DATE"

6) A LARGE TOWN

DOWN

7) ONES WHO BUILD

8) TALL, FLAT STRUCTURES SURROUNDING ANCIENT CITIES - RHYMES WITH "CALLS"

9) OPPOSITE OF DAY

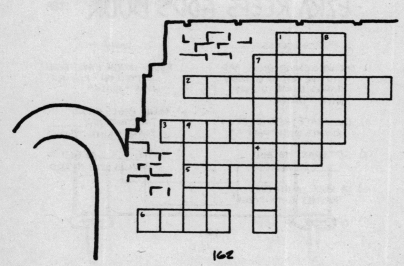

EZRA READS THE LAW

NEHEMIAH 8, 13

ACROSS

1) OPPOSITE OF PUSH

2) THE PEOPLE MADE A _____ TO GOD (A VOW).

3) _____ READ THE LAW TO THE PEOPLE.

DOWN

1) HUMAN BEINGS, NATION, RACE - RHYMES WITH "STEEPLE"

4) OPPOSITE OF SAD

5) A TALL STAND FROM WHICH A SPEAKER TALKS

6) OPPOSITE OF WORK - RHYMES WITH "BEST"

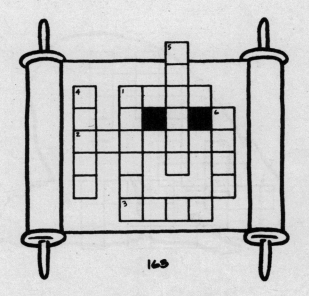

THE EVIL HAMAN

ESTHER 3

ACROSS

1) OPPOSITE OF LOVE

2) YOU WEAR A _____ ON YOUR HEAD (RHYMES WITH "CAT").

3) OPPOSITE OF UP

4) A RULE, DECREE, STATUTE - RHYMES WITH "PAW"

DOWN

1) _____ HATED THE JEWS (RHYMES WITH "CANAAN").

3) OPPOSITE OF MOM

5) MORDECAI _____ BY THE GATE EVERY DAY (RHYMES WITH "CAT").

6) CHILDREN OF ISRAEL, HEBREWS

7) HAMAN DEMANDED THAT EVERYONE _____ DOWN TO HIM (RHYMES WITH "HOW").

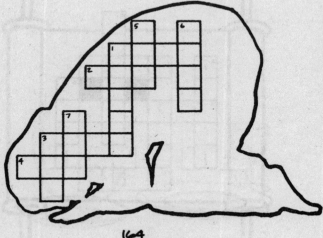

164

ESTHER TELLS
OF
HAMAN'S PLOT

ACROSS

1) ESTHER _____ HER
   PEOPLE FROM HAMAN'S
   EVIL PLOT (RHYMES
   WITH "PAVED").

2) _____ WAS GOING TO
   KILL THE JEWS.

3) OPPOSITE OF HIM

4) THE CHILDREN OF
   ISRAEL,
   HEBREWS

DOWN

5) GOD USED QUEEN
   _____ TO
   SAVE THE
   JEWS.

6) A LARGE MEAL
   LATER IN THE
   DAY - RHYMES
   WITH "THINNER"

165

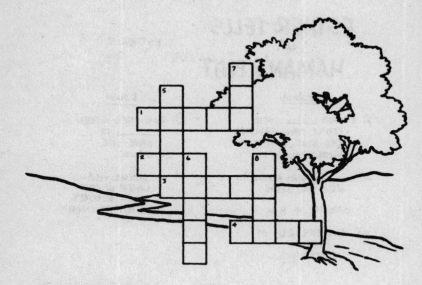

PSALM 1

ACROSS

1) OPPOSITE OF SAD

2) THE NUMBER AFTER NINE

3) LONG, FLOWING BODY OF WATER - RHYMES WITH "QUIVER"

4) A UNIT OF FOLIAGE OF A PLANT - RHYMES WITH "THIEF"

DOWN

5) LIQUID THAT FLOWS IN A RIVER

6) OPPOSITE OF DAY

7) OPPOSITE OF NIGHT

8) VERY TALL PLANT WITH A TRUNK - RHYMES WITH "FREE"

K66

PSALM 42

ACROSS

1) WE EAT ____ TO LIVE.

2) ____ FLOWS OUT OF A FOUNTAIN.

3) WITHOUT WATER TO DRINK YOU HAVE ____ (RHYMES WITH "FIRST")

DOWN

3) ____ FALL FROM OUR EYES WHEN WE CRY.

4) WATER SHOOTING UP OR OUT - RHYMES WITH "MOUNTAIN"

5) A GRACEFUL ANIMAL WITH ANTLERS - RHYMES WITH "FEAR"

6) SMALL RIVER OR BROOK - RHYMES WITH "CREAM"

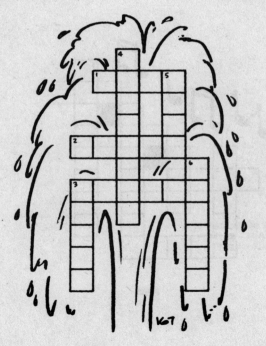

PSALM 117

ACROSS

1) OPPOSITE OF HERS

2) "PRAISE THE _____"

3) TO WORSHIP, ADORE, EXTOL - RHYMES WITH "RAISE"

4) "_____ THY MOTHER AND THY FATHER"

DOWN

5) BENEVOLENCE, THE QUALITY OF BEING KIND

6) ETERNITY

7) OPPOSITE OF HER

8) OPPOSITE OF LIE

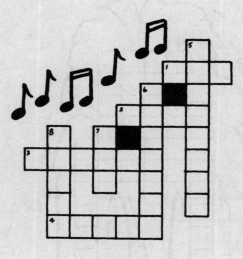

168

THE VIRTUOUS WOMAN

PROVERBS 31:10-31

ACROSS

1) LABORS, EFFORTS, TASKS
   RHYMES WITH "PERKS"

2) THE LIMBS THAT EXTEND
   FROM THE SHOULDERS

3) OPPOSITE OF BAD

4) "CLAP YOUR _____."
   RHYMES WITH
   "SANDS"

5) A WOMAN IS MARRIED
   TO HER _____.

DOWN

1) OPPOSITE OF MAN

4) A BUILDING
   PEOPLE LIVE IN

6) OPPOSITE OF
   WEAK

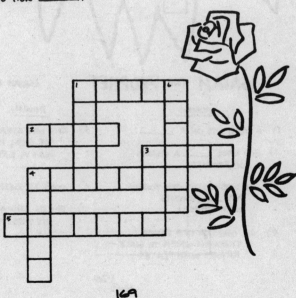

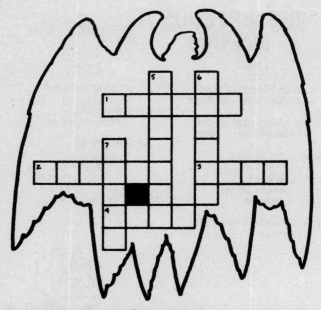

ISAIAH the PROPHET

ISAIAH 6

ACROSS

1) A KING SITS ON A _____.

2) GOD GAVE _____ A VISION OF PROPHESY.

3) WE SPEAK WITH OUR TONGUE AND ___ (RHYMES WITH "SIPS").

4) AN OPENING IN A FENCE THROUGH WHICH TO WALK - RHYMES WITH "LATE"

DOWN

5) ONE WHO SPEAKS FOR GOD; ISAIAH WAS A GREAT _____.

6) GOD'S MESSENGERS

7) BIRDS AND ANGELS USE THESE TO FLY.

170

THE SOARING EAGLE

ISAIAH 40:31

ACROSS

1) THE SPACE OVERHEAD, THE HEAVENS - RHYMES WITH "FLY"

2) TO MOVE AS FAST AS YOU CAN BY FOOT - RHYMES WITH "FUN"

3) THE FINAL AIM IN A CONTEST, TO GET A POINT - RHYMES WITH "SOUL"

4) OPPOSITE OF WEAK

DOWN

1) TO RISE UP HIGH, "_____ LIKE AN EAGLE" - RHYMES WITH "POOR"

5) BIRDS FLAP THEIR _____.

6) THE OPPOSITE ONE OF TWO - "NOT THAT ONE. THE _____ ONE."

7) "PRAISE THE _____."

8) LARGE BIRD OF PREY, SYMBOL OF THE USA

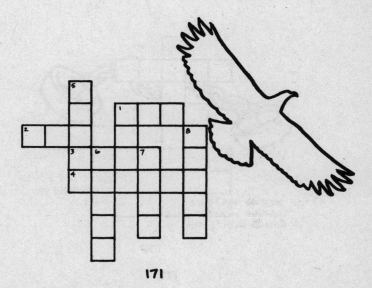

JEREMIAH IN PRISON

JEREMIAH 37-38:13

ACROSS

1) TO TALK, TO UTTER SPEECH - RHYMES WITH "PEAK"

2) OPPOSITE OF SHE

3) OPPOSITE OF UP

4) A PLACE WHERE PEOPLE ARE HELD CAPTIVE, A DUNGEON - RHYMES WITH "RISEN"

DOWN

4) A DEEP HOLE IN THE GROUND - RHYMES WITH "PIT"

5) _____ WAS THROWN IN PRISON.

6) FALSE GODS

7) OPPOSITE OF OFF

EZEKIEL'S VISION
EZEKIEL 37:1-14

ACROSS

1) OPPOSITE OF FOUND

2) THE LOWLAND BETWEEN TWO MOUNTAINS - RHYMES WITH "GALLEY"

3) ONLY A _____ COULD OFFER SACRIFICES TO THE LORD.

4) THE PARTS OF OUR SKELETON - RHYMES WITH "STONES"

DOWN

5) OPPOSITE OF DEAD

6) GOD GAVE _____ A VISION.

7) ANTICIPATION OF A GOOD THING - RHYMES WITH "SOAP"

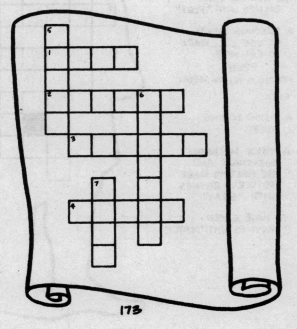

DANIEL AND THE KING'S DREAM

ACROSS

1) YOU WEAR SHOES ON YOUR _____.

2) THE PLATE _____ WHEN I DROPPED IT.- RHYMES WITH "JOKE"

3) _____ COULD TELL THE MEANINGS OF THE KING'S DREAMS.

4) THE COLOR OF CLAY- RHYMES WITH "PLAY"

5) A PRECIOUS METAL - WE USE _____ WARE TO EAT WITH.

DOWN

4) PRECIOUS YELLOW METAL

6) ROCK

7) A VISION DURING SLEEP

8) A THICK, MOLDABLE SUBSTANCE, CAN BE FIRED TO MAKE POTTERY- RHYMES WITH "GRAY"

9) TO HAVE EATEN - RHYMES WITH "PLATE"

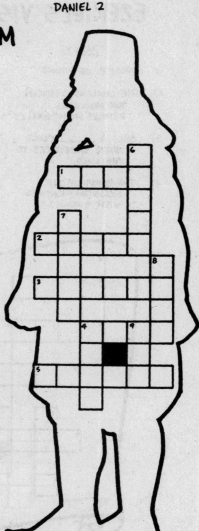

174

DANIEL AND THE LIONS
DANIEL 6

ACROSS

1) OPPOSITE OF CLOSED

2) THE LIONS DID NOT HARM _____.

3) AN OPENING THROUGH THE WALL TO THE OUTSIDE TO LET IN LIGHT AND FRESH AIR.

4) TO GET DOWN ON YOUR KNEES - RHYMES WITH "FEEL"

DOWN

5) A CAVE WHERE THE LIONS LIVED - RHYMES WITH "PEN"

6) TO TALK TO GOD

7) OPPOSITE OF MANY

8) KINGS OF BEASTS

9) A FEMALE DEER

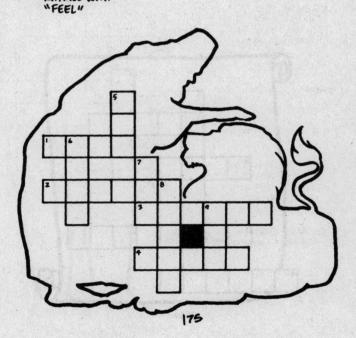

ZACHARIAS

LUKE 1:5-25

ACROSS

1) A MESSENGER OF GOD, GABRIEL, THE _____

2) _____ THE BAPTIST

3) KIDS

4) ZACHARIAS WAS A _____ WHO SERVED IN THE TEMPLE (RHYMES WITH "FEAST").

DOWN

5) FOR A TIME ZACHARIAS COULD NOT _____ (TALK).

6) AN ANGEL APPEARED TO _____ (JOHN THE BAPTIST'S FATHER).

7) OPPOSITE OF YOUNG

8) A BOY CHILD - RHYMES WITH "FUN" OPPOSITE OF DAUGHTER

176

MARY VISITS ELIZABETH LUKE 1:39-45

ACROSS

1) THE CHILD OF ONE'S UNCLE OR AUNT - RHYMES WITH "DOZEN"

2) MARY WENT TO VISIT HER COUSIN_____.

3) GLADNESS, GREAT HAPPINESS

4) ELIZABETH WOULD HAVE A _____ BOY (RHYMES WITH "MAYBE")

DOWN

5) TO GO SEE SOMEONE FOR A SHORT STAY

6) THE MOTHER OF JESUS

7) SET APART TO GOD, _____ OF HOLIES

THE ANGELS
TELL THE SHEPHERDS

LUKE 2 : 8-20

ACROSS

1) GREAT GLADNESS, HAPPINESS

2) THOSE WHO CARE FOR SHEEP

3) "GLORY TO _____ IN THE HIGHEST"

DOWN

1) _____ WAS THE NEWBORN SAVIOR.

2) TO LOOK WITH YOUR EYES - RHYMES WITH "BEE"

4) GOD'S MESSENGERS

5) OPPOSITE OF DAY

6) FEARFUL

7) THE SPACE HIGH OVERHEAD, THE HEAVENS - RHYMES WITH "PIE"

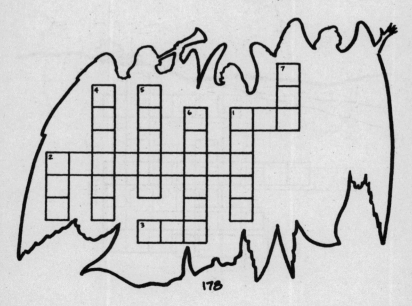

178

THE WISE MEN

MATTHEW 2:1-12

ACROSS

1) PRECIOUS YELLOW METAL

2) OPPOSITE OF WEST

3) IF YOU HAVE WISDOM, YOU ARE _____.

4) PRESENTS

5) MOTHER OF JESUS

6) THE MAN WHO RULES OVER A COUNTRY

DOWN

5) OPPOSITE OF WOMEN

7) THE BUILDING PEOPLE LIVE IN - RHYMES WITH "MOUSE"

8) HUMP-BACKED DESERT CREATURES

9) SMALL CITY - RHYMES WITH "DOWN"

10) BRIGHT POINT OF LIGHT IN THE NIGHT SKY

11) THE SPACE OVERHEAD, THE HEAVENS - RHYMES WITH "PIE"

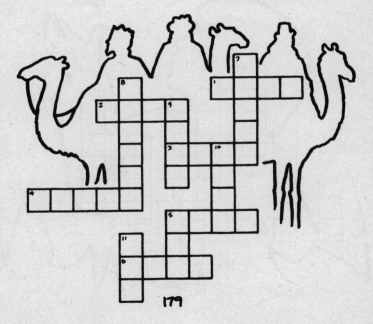

179

JESUS AS A BOY

LUKE 2:39-40

ACROSS

1) AN ANGEL TOLD JOSEPH TO ___ BACK TO ISRAEL (OPPOSITE OF STOP).

2) IF YOU HAVE WISDOM, YOU ARE _____ (RHYMES WITH "EYES").

3) OPPOSITE OF GIRL

4) FATHER, SON, HOLY ___

DOWN

1) GOT BIGGER

3) A CREATURE WITH FEATHERS AND WINGS

5) THE SON OF GOD

6) THE LAND WHERE PHARAOHS RULED - MOSES LED THE PEOPLE OUT OF _____.

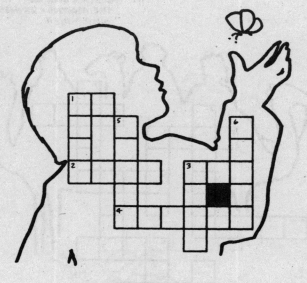

JOHN the BAPTIST

LUKE 3:1-11

ACROSS

1) A DRY, BARREN LAND

2) _____ THE BAPTIST

3) TO TURN AWAY FROM SIN AND DO RIGHT- RHYMES WITH "RESENT"

4) OPPOSITE OF SHE

DOWN

5) JOHN WORE CLOTHES MADE OF ANIMAL _____ (RHYMES WITH "THIN").

6) ONE WHO SPEAKS FOR GOD

7) JOHN ATE LOCUSTS AND WILD _____ (THE SWEET SYRUP BEES MAKE).

JESUS IN THE DESERT

MATTHEW 4:1-11

ACROSS

1) ROCKS

2) SATAN IS THE _____.
   (RHYMES WITH
   "LEVEL")

3) _____ WAS TEMPTED
   IN THE DESERT.

4) SATAN SAID, "IF YOU
   ARE THE SON OF GOD,
   MAKE THESE STONES
   INTO LOAVES OF _____."

DOWN

2) A BARREN, DRY
   LAND

5) THERE IS ONLY _____
   GOD (THE NUMBER
   BEFORE TWO).

6) WICKED, BAD

7) OPPOSITE OF SIT -
   RHYMES WITH
   "HAND"

182

PETER, PHILIP AND NATHANAEL

JOHN 1: 40-51

ACROSS

1) ONES WHO FOLLOW

2) GOD'S DWELLING PLACE ON HIGH

3) MORE THAN ONE MAN - OPPOSITE OF WOMEN

4) OPPOSITE OF OFF

DOWN

1) JESUS NOW HAD _____ FOLLOWERS (THE NUMBER AFTER FOUR).

5) TO PLACE YOUR FAITH IN SOMETHING - "I _____ IN GOD." (RHYMES WITH "RELIEVE")

6) OPPOSITE OF CLOSED

7) A VERY TALL PLANT WITH A TRUNK - RHYMES WITH "FREE"

JESUS CLEANS OUT THE TEMPLE

JOHN 2:12-16

ACROSS

1) THE NUMBER AFTER NINE

2) TO PURCHASE - RHYMES WITH "MY"

3) HOUSE OF WORSHIP

4) OPPOSITE OF BUY

DOWN

1) FLAT PIECES OF FURNITURE ON LEGS - RHYMES WITH "CABLES"

5) WE USE _____ TO BUY THINGS

6) A LION TAMER USES A _____ AND A CHAIR TO CONTROL THE LIONS (RHYMES WITH "RIP")

7) ANGRY

8) OPPOSITE OF IN

184

HEROD PUTS JOHN IN PRISON

LUKE 3:18-20

ACROSS

1) KING HEROD PUT JOHN THE BAPTIST IN A PRISON FAR _____.

2) OPPOSITE OF LOVED

3) _____ THE BAPTIST

DOWN

2) KING _____ RULED OVER GALILEE.

4) A MAN IS MARRIED TO HIS _____.

5) OPPOSITE OF NO

6) TO USE YOUR BRAIN, MEDITATE - RHYMES WITH "DRINK"

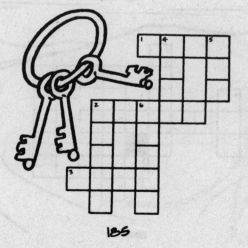

185

THE NOBLEMAN'S SON   JOHN 4:46-54

ACROSS

1) THERE ARE 24 OF
   THESE IN ONE DAY,
   60 MINUTES IS
   ONE _____.

2) AN IMPORTANT, RICH
   MAN OF HIGH RANK

3) THE SON OF GOD

DOWN

1) CURED

4) OPPOSITE OF DAUGHTER,
   A BOY CHILD

5) WHEN A PERSON IS
   HOT FROM AN
   ILLNESS, HE HAS
   A _____

6) STREETS, WELL-TRAVELED
   PATHS - RHYMES
   WITH "TOADS"

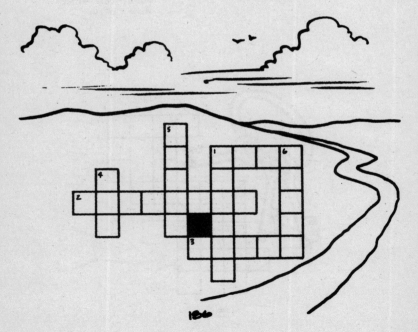

186

THE FISHERMEN

LUKE 5:1-11

ACROSS

1) A LARGE BODY OF WATER - RHYMES WITH "TEA"

2) A WEB OF CORD FISHERMAN USE TO CATCH FISH - RHYMES WITH "PET"

3) OPPOSITE OF EMPTY

4) VESSELS TO CARRY MEN ON WATER - RHYMES WITH "COATS"

DOWN

3) FINNED CREATURES THAT LIVE IN WATER

5) OPPOSITE OF FEW

6) ONE LESS THAN THREE

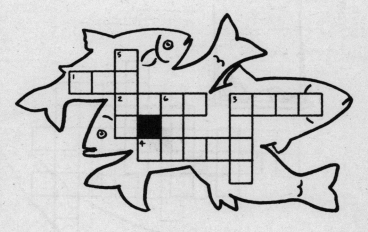

187

THROUGH the ROOF

LUKE 5:17-26

ACROSS

1) THE TOP OF A HOUSE

2) AN OWL ASKS, "____?"

3) CURED

4) TO BREAK GOD'S LAW

8) PLACE, LOCATION
"____ WERE YOU BORN?" –
RHYMES WITH "HAIR"

DOWN

2) TO STROLL – TRAVEL BY FOOT – RHYMES WITH "TALK"

5) LARGE GROUP OF PEOPLE – RHYMES WITH "LOUD"

6) TO PARDON – ENDS WITH "GIVE"

7) WE SLEEP IN A ____.

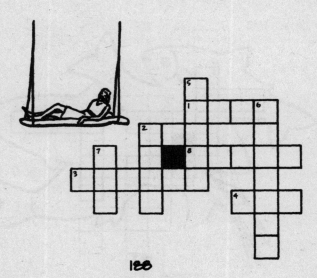

188

JESUS, LORD of the SABBATH

ACROSS

1) OPPOSITE OF SHE

2) THE SEEDS OF CEREAL PLANTS LIKE WHEAT - RHYMES WITH "TRAIN"

3) DEEP HOLE IN THE GROUND - RHYMES WITH "SIT"

4) RULE, STATUTE - RHYMES WITH "PAW"

5) WE HAVE A _____ AT THE END OF EACH ARM.

DOWN

1) WHEN YOU DON'T EAT, YOU GET _____.

6) THE LORD'S DAY, DAY OF REST

7) FARMERS GROW CROPS IN THEIR _____.

8) TO HAVE EATEN - RHYMES WITH "GATE"

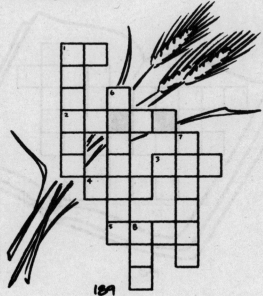

189

THE TWELVE APOSTLES LUKE 6:12-16

ACROSS

1) OPPOSITE OF FALSE

2) THE TAX COLLECTOR

3) JESUS CHOSE TWELVE _____.

4) HIS NAME MEANS "ROCK"

DOWN

1) THE NUMBER AFTER ELEVEN

5) OPPOSITE OF BOTTOM

6) OPPOSITE OF HERS (BELONGING TO HIM)

7) THE APOSTLE WHO WOULD BETRAY JESUS.

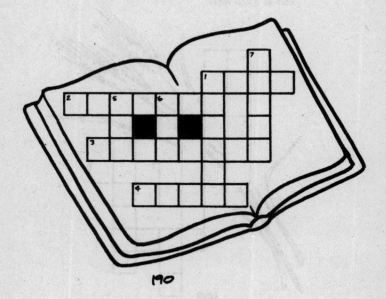

190

THE SOWER

LUKE 8:4-15

ACROSS

1) TO SCATTER SEEDS - RHYMES WITH "TOW"

2) OPPOSITE OF GOOD

3) THE DIRT WE WALK ON, THE EARTH - RHYMES WITH "FOUND"

4) A PLANT GROWS FROM A _____ (RHYMES WITH "FEED").

DOWN

2) WINGED, FEATHERED FLYING CREATURES

3) OPPOSITE OF BAD

5) ROSES HAVE SHARP _____.

6) STONE - RHYMES WITH "CLOCK"

191

PARABLES of JESUS

MATTHEW 13:24-52

ACROSS

1) STORIES JESUS TOLD TO SHOW A TRUTH

2) RICHES, VALUABLES - "BURIED _____"

3) THE GRAIN WE MAKE FLOUR FROM - RHYMES WITH "SEAT"

4) A PLANT GROWS FROM A _____ (RHYMES WITH "FEED")

DOWN

5) KETCHUP AND _____ GO GREAT ON A HOT DOG (RHYMES WITH "CUSTARD").

6) A BEAUTIFUL FLOWER WITH THORNS - RHYMES WITH "HOSE"

7) WINGED, FEATHERED FLYING CREATURES

8) A VERY TALL PLANT WITH A TRUNK - RHYMES WITH "FREE"

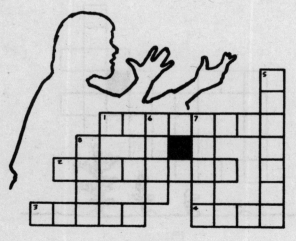

192

A GIRL
LIVES
AGAIN

MARK 5:35-43

ACROSS

1) THE GIRL'S PARENTS WERE _____ THAT SHE WAS DEAD (OPPOSITE OF HAPPY).

2) NOT ALIVE

3) TO BE IN THE STATE OF SLEEP

4) OPPOSITE OF FALL – JESUS TOLD THE GIRL TO _____ UP (RHYMES WITH EYES).

DOWN

5) JESUS TOOK HER BY THE _____ (RHYMES WITH "SAND").

6) _____ RAISED THE GIRL FROM THE DEAD.

7) SHE WAS _____ YEARS OLD (ONE MORE THAN ELEVEN).

8) ALL THE PEOPLE MADE A LOUD _____ OUTSIDE (OPPOSITE OF LAUGH).

JESUS WALKS ON WATER   MATTHEW 14:22-27

ACROSS

1) TRAVELED BY FOOT, STROLLED - RHYMES WITH "TALKED"

2) TO BE AFRAID IS TO BE FULL OF _____. (RHYMES WITH "HEAR")

3) A VIOLENT DISTURBANCE IN THE WEATHER - RHYMES WITH "FORM"

DOWN

1) JESUS WALKED ON _____.

4) TRANSPARENT - THE WATER WAS CRYSTAL _____. (RHYMES WITH "FEAR"

5) THE SON OF GOD

6) A VESSEL THAT CARRIES MEN UPON THE WATER - RHYMES WITH "COAT"

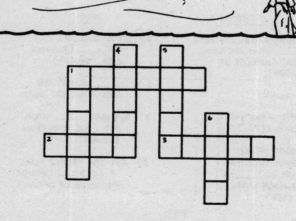

JESUS TRANSFIGURED

MARK 9:2-10

ACROSS

1) A TALL PEAK OF LAND

2) GOD SAID, "THIS IS MY BELOVED _____"

3) WHITE FLAKES THAT FALL FROM THE SKY IN WINTER

DOWN

1) THE MAN GOD CHOSE TO LEAD THE PEOPLE OUT OF EGYPT-RHYMES WITH "HOSES"

4) THE DISCIPLE CALLED "THE ROCK"

5) OPPOSITE OF LOW

6) MIDDAY- RHYMES WITH "SOON"

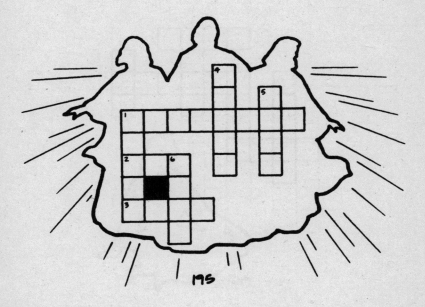

195

MARY AND MARTHA

LUKE 10:38-42

ACROSS

1) OPPOSITE OF UP

2) _____ WAS TOO BUSY WORKING. (MARY'S SISTER)

3) ACTIVE, DOING MANY THINGS - RHYMES WITH "DIZZY"

DOWN

2) _____ SAT AT THE FEET OF JESUS AND LISTENED TO HIS WORDS. (MARTHA'S SISTER)

4) TO LABOR, EXERT EFFORT - RHYMES WITH "PERK"

5) THE SON OF GOD

6) OPPOSITE OF STAND

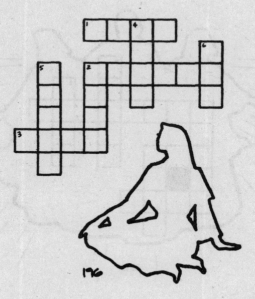

196

ANSWERS

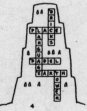

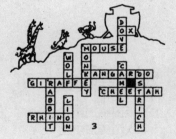

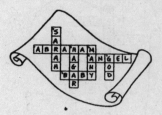

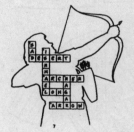

ANSWERS

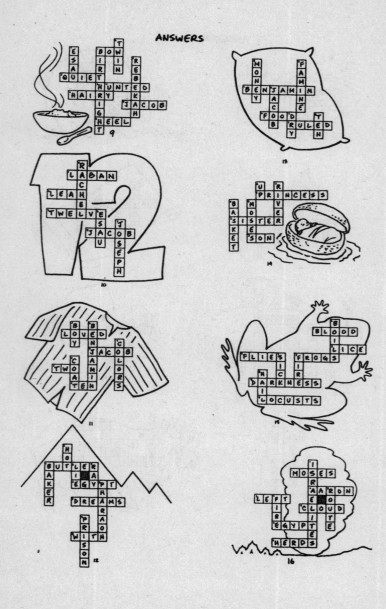

ANSWERS

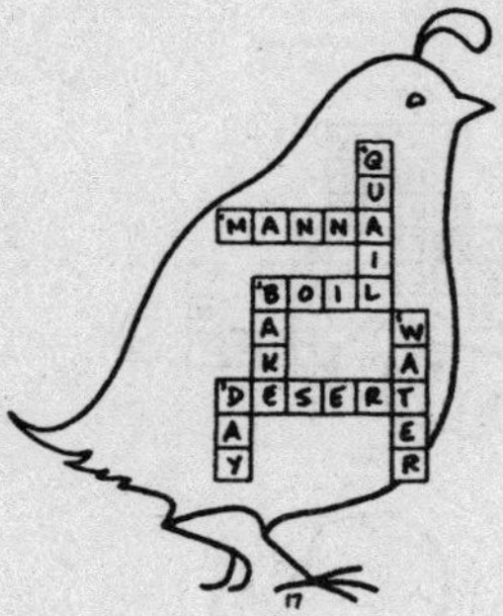

QUAIL
MANNA
BOIL
BAKE
DESERT
DAY
WATER

17

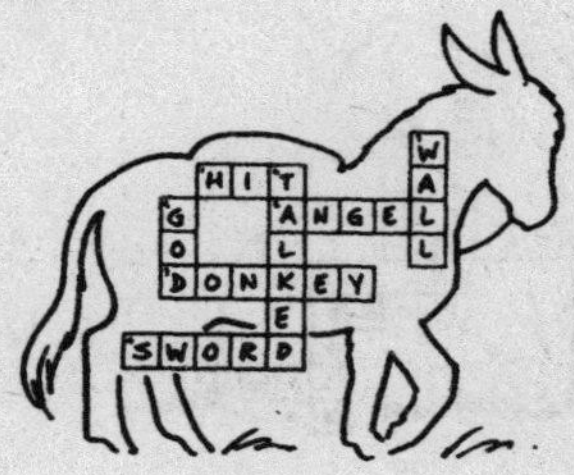

WALL
HIT
ANGEL
GOD
DONKEY
TALKED
SWORD

21

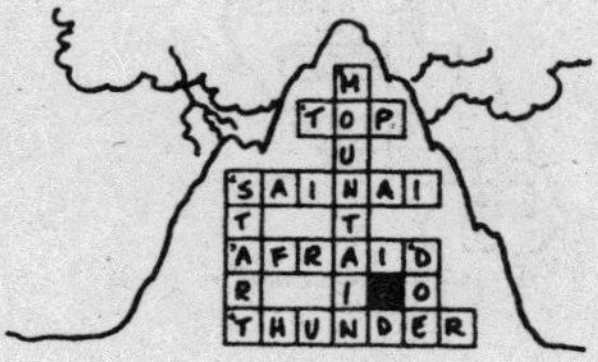

MOUNTAIN
TOP
SAINAI
START
AFRAID
DOE
THUNDER

18

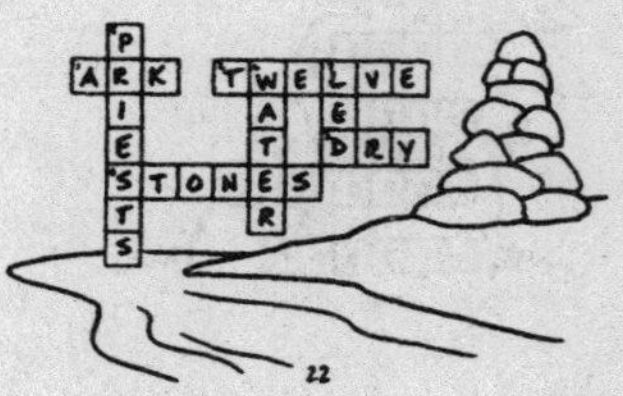

PRIESTS
ARK
TWELVE
WATER
LED
DRY
STONES

22

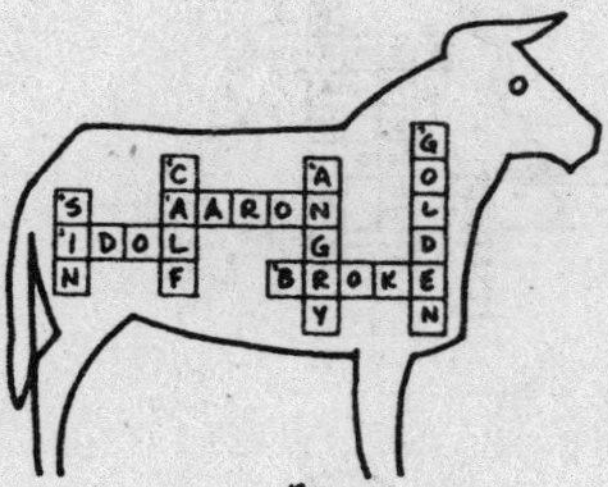

GOLDEN
CALF
AARON
ANGRY
SIN
IDOL
BROKE

19

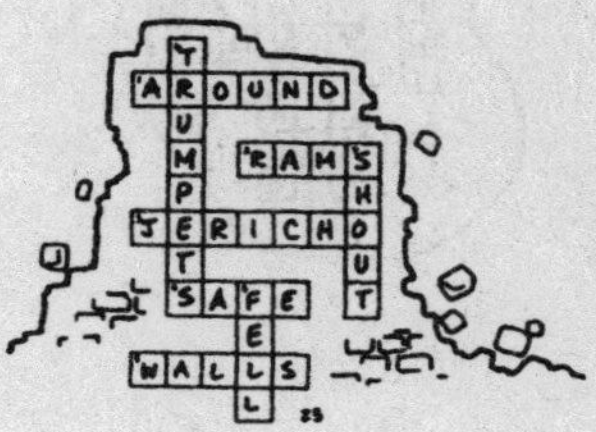

TRUMPETS
AROUND
RAMS
SHOUT
JERICHO
SAFE
FELL
WALLS

23

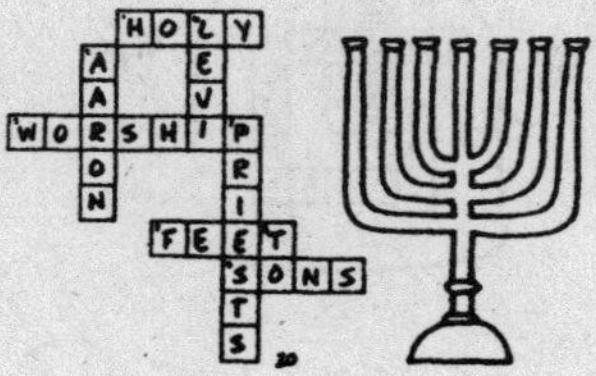

HOLY
AARON
LEVI
WORSHIP
PRIESTS
FEET
SONS

20

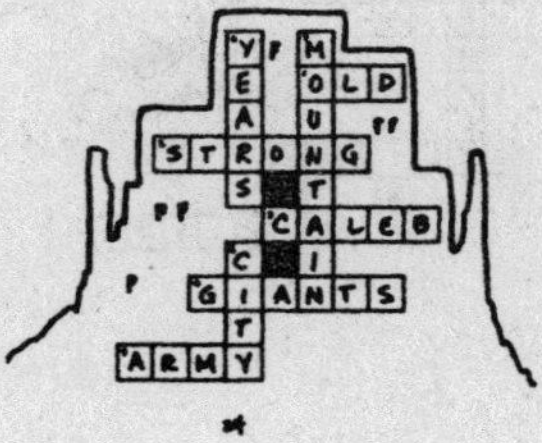

YEARS
MOUNT
OLD
STRONG
CALEB
CITY
GIANTS
ARMY

24

ANSWERS

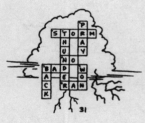

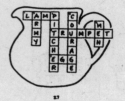

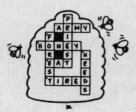

ANSWERS

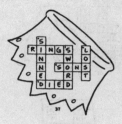

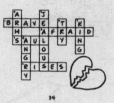

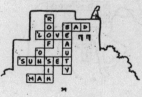

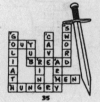

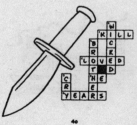

ANSWERS

41

LIFE
R Y
I O
HELP
N U
D
F
GOODS
O
BEDS

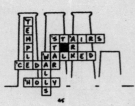

45

TEMPLE
E   T
M   STAIRS
P   R
L   WALKED
CEDAR L
A Y
HOLY S

42

THRONE KING
C   A
CROWN AGE
S O   S
PEACE H

46

NA
PHARAOH
WICKED LD
IDOLS O
E U
EGYPT

43

OLD
I
SOLOMON
O U E
N L X
PRIEST
O
DE

47

SKI
M I
RAVENS
I N
RAIN
J
BEARD

44

A W
N RICHES
S A K
WE S
SERVE
R O
PRAY

49

RI
IDOL FALSE
OXEN FIRE
A L R
L ALTAR O
M

ANSWERS

44

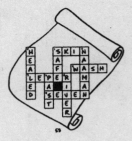

53

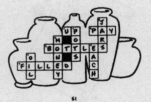

50

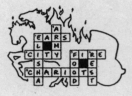

54

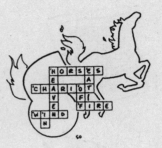

51

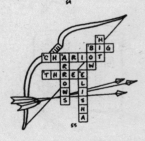

55

52

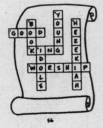

56

ANSWERS

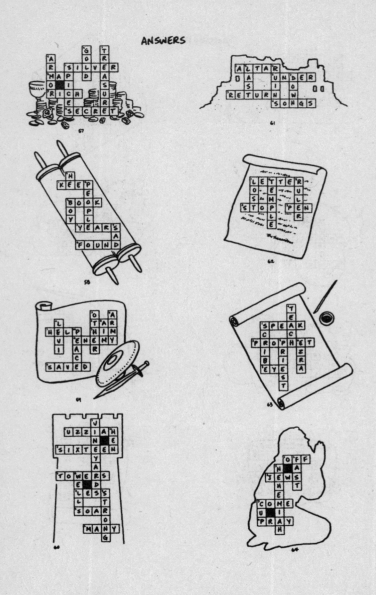

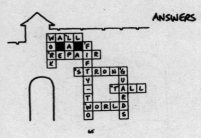

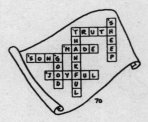

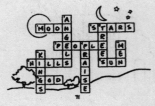

ANSWERS

Puzzle 78 (house/stable):
WHEN / BORN / SON / GOD / COUNSELOR / PRINCE / WONDERFUL / FOUND / CHILD

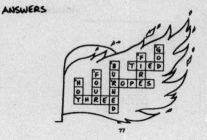

Puzzle 77:
GOD / FIRE / TIED / BURN / ROPES / NOT / FOUR / THREE / BURNED

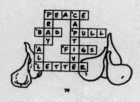

Puzzle 74:
PEACE / EAT / BAD / FULL / FIGS / ALL / LETTER

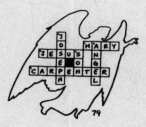

Puzzle 78 (whale):
B / N / SEA / FISH / OIL / IN / SWALLOWED / IN / V / WATER / HH / HH

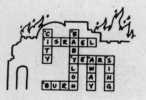

Puzzle 75:
CITY / ISRAEL / BABYLON / YEARS / SING / BURN / WAY

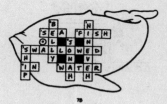

Puzzle 79:
YOUNG / MARY / JESUS / CARPENTER

Puzzle 76 (jug):
YOUNG / PLUM / KING / FOUT / DANIEL

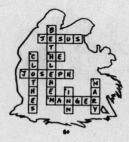

Puzzle 80:
B / JESUS / THE / CLOTHES / JOSEPH / MANGER / MARY

ANSWERS

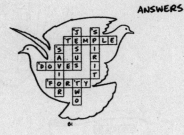

81

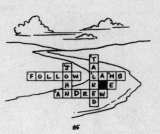

85

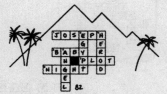

82

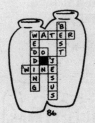

86

83

87

84

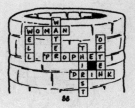

88

ANSWERS

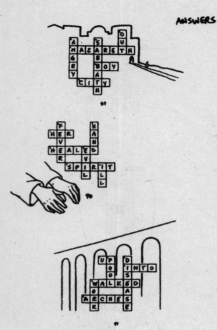

ANSWERS

99

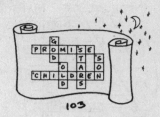

103

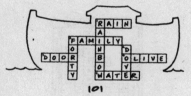

100

104

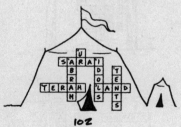

101

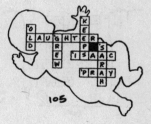

105

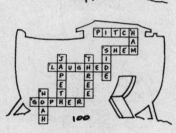

102

106

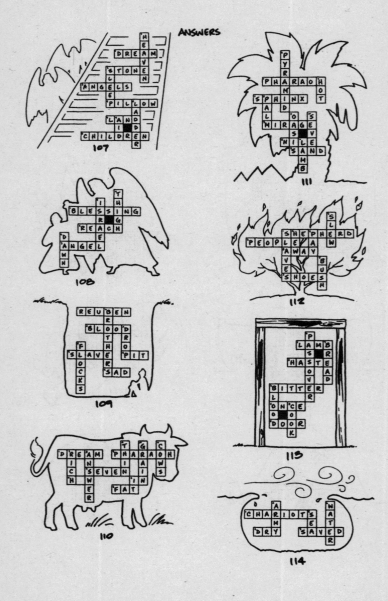

ANSWERS

107

H
DREAM
HEAVEN
STONE
ANGELS
PILLOW
LAND
CHILDREN

111

PYR
PHARAOH HOT
SPHINX
MIRAGE
NILE
SAND

108

BLESSING
REACH
ANGEL
DAMN

112

SHEPHERD
PEOPLE AWAY
SHOES
BUSH

109

REUBEN
BLOOD
PIT
SLAVE
SAD
FLOCKS

113

LAMBS
HASTE
BITTER
ONCE
DOOR

110

DREAM PHARAOH
SEVEN
FAT

114

CHARIOTS WATER
DRY SAVED

ANSWERS

115

119

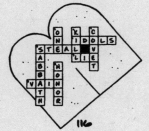

116

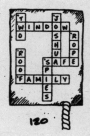

120

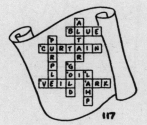

117

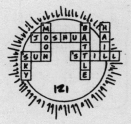

121

118

122

ANSWERS

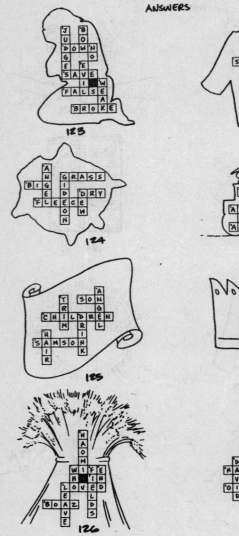

123

```
J   B
JUDGE  DOWN
E   O
SAVE
I W
FALSE
E A
BROKE
```
(puzzle 123)

127
```
      C
   E  OAT
   SISTERS
   A  G
   MEOW
   U  E
   YEAR
   L
```

124
```
A
NGE  GRASS
BIG  I  DRY
E  D E
FLEECEW
O  N
```

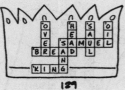

128
```
WAGON
L  OX
AFRAID
A  D
ARK
```

125
```
      A
   TRI  SON  N
      M  G
CHILDREN
   H  I
   SAMSON K
   I
   R
```

129
```
O  H  S  O
VE RE A IL
BREAD
   N
KING
```

126
```
   NAOMI
   WIFE
   H  IN
LOVED
E  L
BOAZ DS
V
E
```

130
```
Y
SH SONGS
   U  A
SEVEN U
D  E GO
HARP
OIL
```

ANSWERS

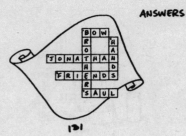

131

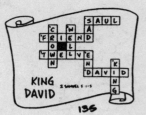

135

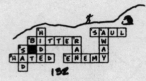

132

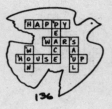

136

138

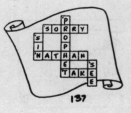

137

134

138

ANSWERS

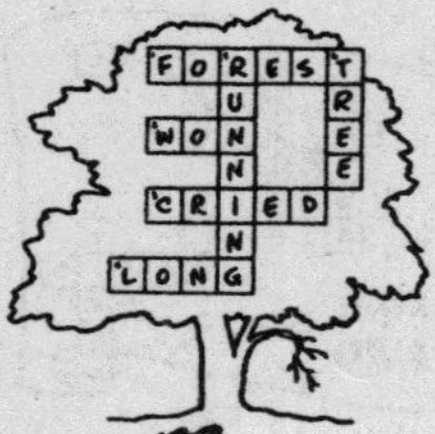
FOREST
TREE
RUNNING
WON
CRIED
LONG

139

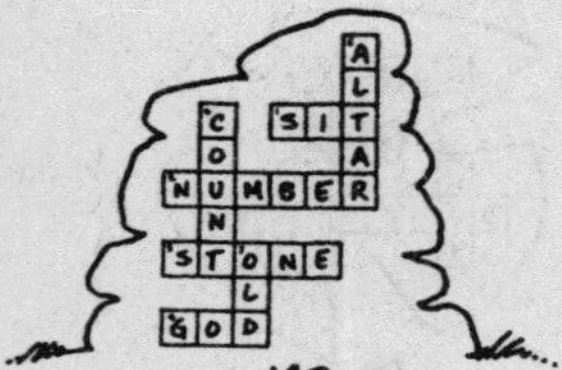
ALTAR
SIT
COUNT
NUMBER
STONE
OLD
GOD

140

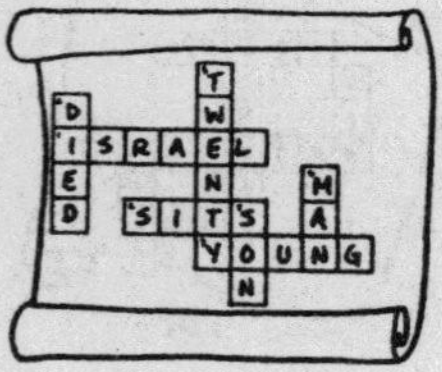
TWENTY
DIED
ISRAEL
MAN
SITS
SON
YOUNG

141

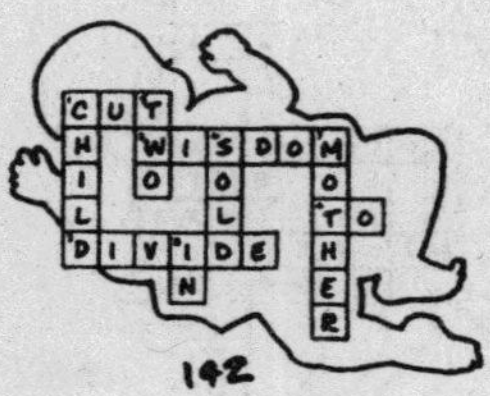
CUT
CHILD
TWO
WISDOM
SOLD
MOTHER
TO
DIVIDE
IN

142

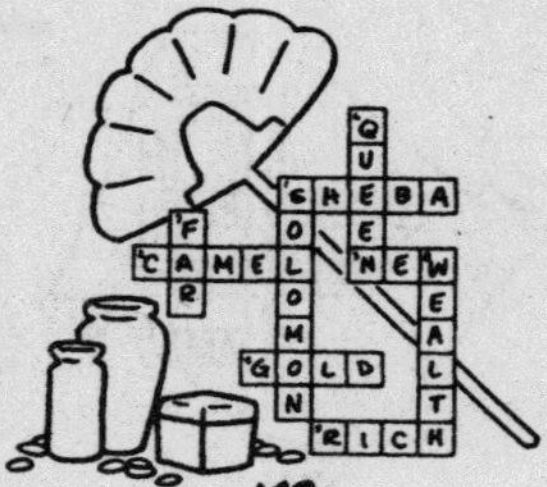
QUEEN
SHEBA
FAR
CAMEL
SOLOMON
NEW
WEALTH
GOLD
RICH

143

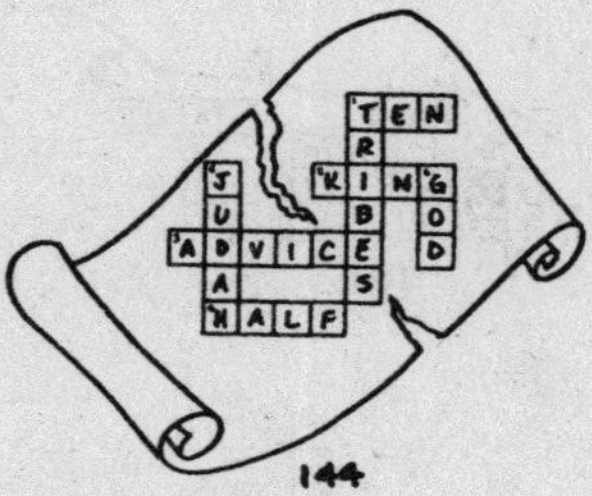
TEN
TRIBES
JUDAH
KING
GOOD
ADVICE
HALF

144

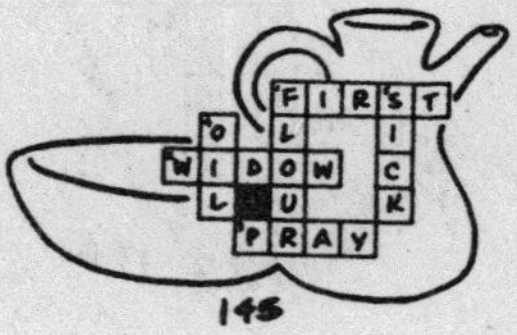
FIRST
FLOUR
SICK
OIL
WIDOW
PRAY

145

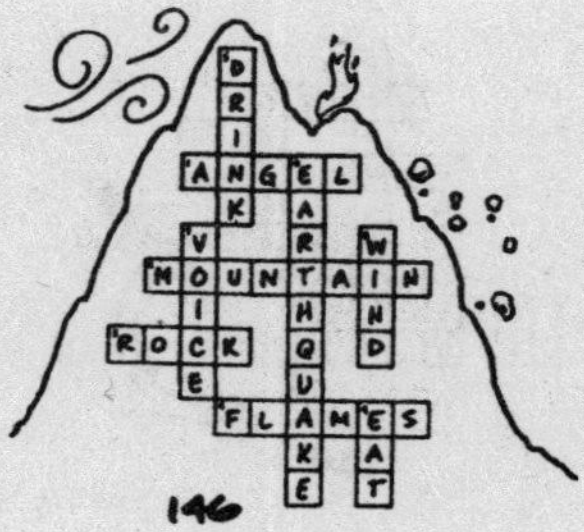
DRINK
ANGEL
EARTHQUAKE
VOICE
WIND
MOUNTAIN
ROCK
FLAMES
EAT

146

ANSWERS

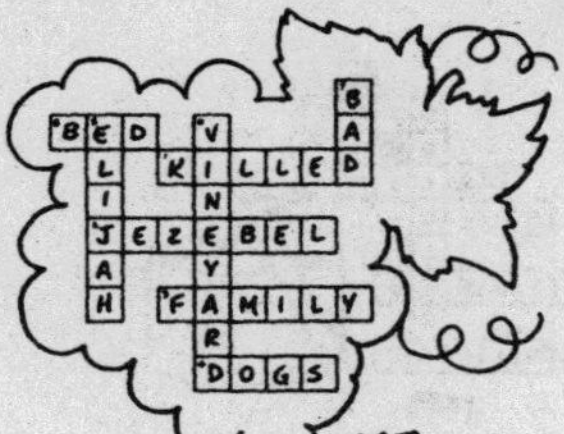
BED
KILLED
JEZEBEL
FAMILY
DOGS

147

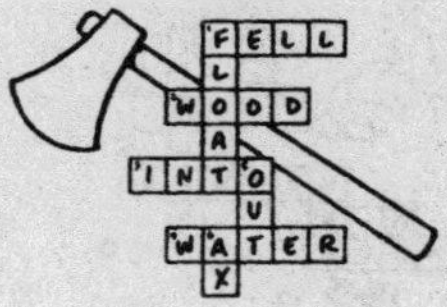
FELL
WOOD
INTO
WATER

151

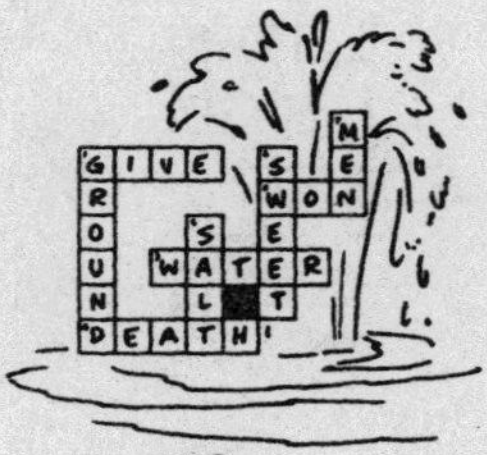
GIVE
WON
WATER
DEATH

148

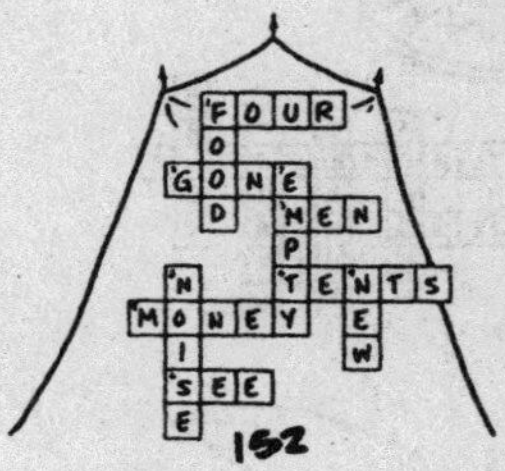
FOUR
GONE
MEN
TENTS
MONEY
SEE

152

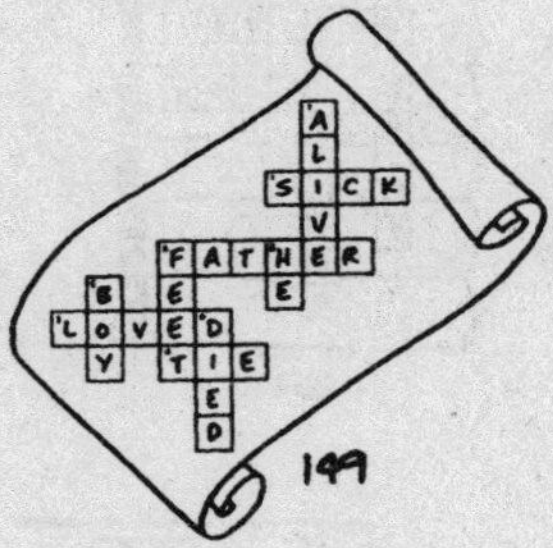
SICK
FATHER
LOVED
TIE

149

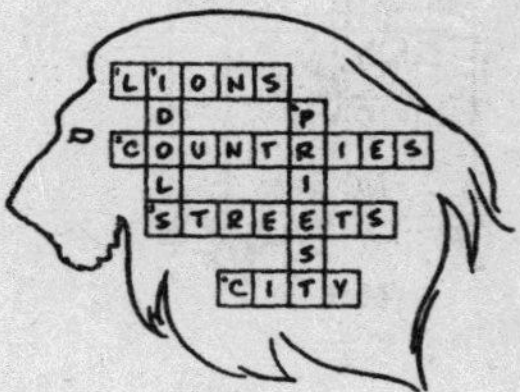
LIONS
COUNTRIES
STREETS
CITY

153

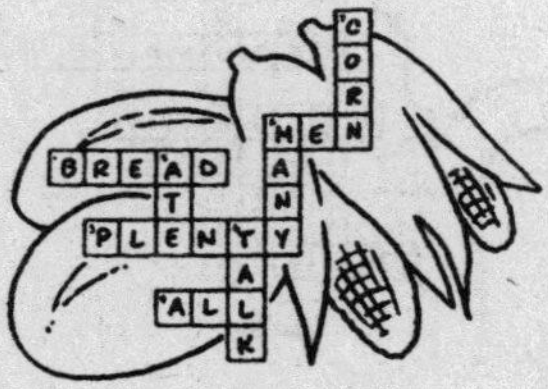
MEN
BREAD
PLENTY
ALL

150

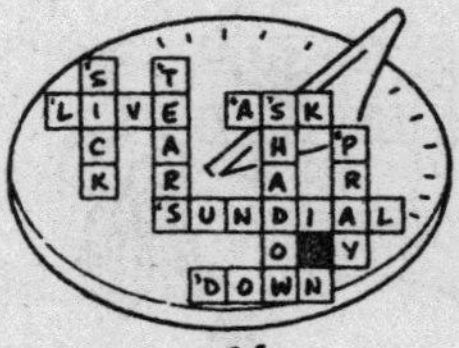
LIVE
ASK
SUNDIAL
DOWN

154

ANSWERS

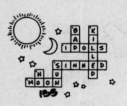

155

BAK / IDOLS / SINNED / NU / MOON

159

G / BELT / U / A / CRIED / SI / LDER / STONES / FIRST

156

S / HE / JEHOSHAPHAT / N / R / A / KINGS / ANX / EY / T

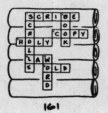

160

PR / JO / HOLY / N / FINISH / PH / ET / GO / WS / LD

157

T / SEVEN / EM / REPAIR / LN / NEW / O / BOX / D

161

SCRIBE / CR / O / COPY / HOLY / K / OR / LAW / OLD / RD

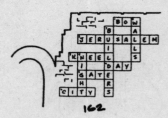

158

INC / R / AFTER / ON / HO / S / LEPROSY / Y / EH / NE / HAD / PRIEST

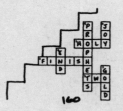

162

BOW / B / JERUSALEM / IL / LS / KNEEL / DAY / IGHT / GATE / CITY

ANSWERS

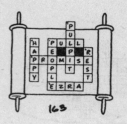

163

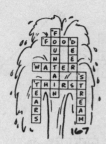

167

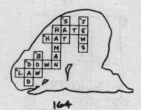

164

168

165

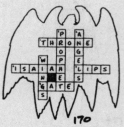

169

166

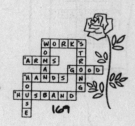

170

171

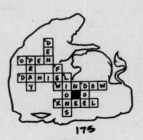

175

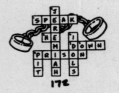

172

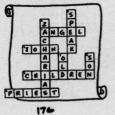

176

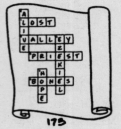

173

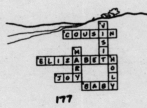

177

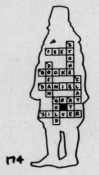

174

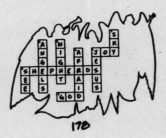

178

ANSWERS

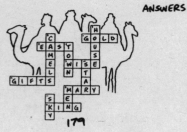

179

CAMELS / EASY / GOLD / HOUSE / TO / WISE / STAR / GIFTS / MARY / SKING / KING

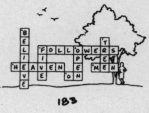

183

BELIEVE / FOLLOWERS / OPEN / SEVEN / HEAVEN / MEN / ON

180

GO / GREW / JESUS / WISE / BOY / SPIRIT / EGYPT

184

MONEY / TEMPLE / TABLE / WHIP / OUT / HEAD / SELL

181

DESERT / PROPHET / HONEY / JOHN / REPENT

185

AWAY / WIFE / YES / WANTED / THINK / WERE / JOHN / DRINK

182

STONES / ONE / OVEN / DEVIL / FELL / JESUS / SET / STAND / BREAD

186

FEVER / HOUR / ROAD / SON / NOBLEMAN / WILL / JESUS / OLD

ANSWERS

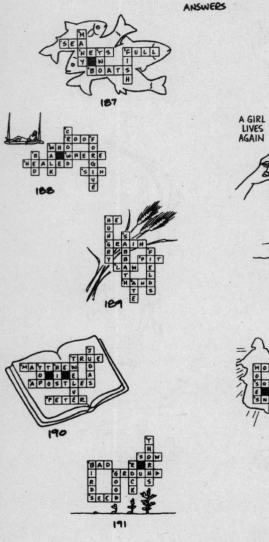

187

SEA / NETS / FULL / FISH / BOATS (with MANY, JOY)

188

CROOF / WHO / WHERE / BA / HEALED / SINGIVE

189

HUNGRY / GAIN / LAW / HANDS / PIT / FIELDS

190

MAYTHEW / TRUE / APOSTLES / PETER

191

BAD / GROUND / SEED / THROWS / ROCK

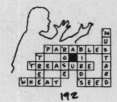

192

PARABLE / TREASURE / WHEAT / MUSTARD SEED

A GIRL
LIVES
AGAIN

193

HAND / DEAD / ASLEEP / ARISE

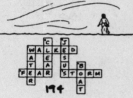

194

WALKED / FEAR / JESUS / STORM / BOAT

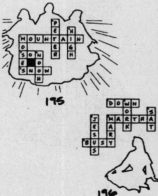

195

MOUNTAIN / SON / SNOW / PETER / HIGH

196

DOWN / MARTHA / JESUS / BUSY / MARY / MARK

Check out these other

KIDS' BIBLE ACTIVITY BOOKS

from

Barbour Publishing

ISBN 978-1-60260-864-1

ISBN 978-1-60260-862-7

ISBN 978-1-60260-861-0

- 224 pages of fun
- Perfect for rainy days, car trips, and Sunday school classes
- Only $3.97 each

Available wherever books are sold.